He models the reality of a marketplace gospel. I recommend his insights as invaluable.

Paul L. Walker, Church of God, Cleveland, Tennessee

He has cast a vision for the future.

W. Thomas Beckner, Taylor University, Fort Wayne, Indiana

Impressive! He presents professional information in a practical way.

LeRoy Attles, St. Paul A. M. E. Church, Cambridge, Massachusetts

Futuring will have a weighty impact on the body of Christ.

Ray Allen Berryhill, Evangel Assembly of God, Chicago, Illinois

I believe in what he has to say, and I am sure you will be blessed and challenged by it.

Gerald Brooks, Grace Outreach Center, Plano, Texas

He is a futuristic, visionary theological thinker for this present age, but he is grounded in practical solutions.

Gerald Durley, Providence Missionary Baptist Church, Atlanta, Georgia

Compelling and practical. He will challenge the sacred cows, the ruts you fall into, and will offer hope for you and your future leadership.

Tim Elmore, Leadership Development, EQUIP, Duluth, Georgia

Anything written by Dr. Chand is a must read. He is unquestionably a leader who understands leading others into the future.

David Graham, Christian City Church, Las Vegas, Nevada

He presents Bible-based principles that prepare us for leadership changes in the future.

Alfred D. Harvey, St. Louis Christian Center, St. Louis, Missouri

When you experience Dr. Chand's writings, your spiritual appetite will be fulfilled.

Darryl L. Hines, Christian Faith Fellowship Church, Milwaukee, Wisconsin

He has the ability to make the complex simple.

Julius R. Malone, New Testament Church of Milwaukee,
Milwaukee, Wisconsin

A unique call of God to motivate and prepare leaders for the twenty-first century.

Kenneth C. Ulmer, Faithful Central Bible Church,
Inglewood, California

If you need to know how to develop a well-defined vision of the future and then build from the ground up, Dr. Chand sets a standard for all of us.

John Wieland, John Wieland Homes, Atlanta, Georgia

He has the uncanny ability to verbalize leadership principles, thus making them proverbs. And with the proverb comes wisdom to lead.

Mark Robertson, chaplain, Grady Health Systems,
Atlanta, Georgia

He challenges all kingdom citizens to stretch, raise the bar, and meet the spiritual and physical needs of a deeply disturbed populace. This book shows you how to do that.

Richard A. Goode, Fellowship of Prayer International Church,
Atlanta, Georgia

Hearing and heeding his words are a must for the society-changing church.

James W. Beaty, Task Force for the Homeless, Atlanta, Georgia

Unwilling to live reactively, he ventures ahead. The result will enable you to catch his enthusiasm to see this world become what God designed.

Arthur Carson, Springfield Missionary Baptist Church,
Atlanta, Georgia

Insightful and humorous, he shares personal experiences to help transform ordinary people into influential leaders.

Stovall Weems, Celebration Church, Jacksonville, Florida

Articulate and witty, giving fresh thought and new perspective. He is futuristic in his approach, confronting current paradigms and challenging his readers.

La Fayette Scales, Rhema Christian Center, Columbus, Ohio

Uncovers profound concepts and delivers them in such a fashion that all can understand.

Marcos Rivera, Primitive Christian Church, New York City

It imparts leadership skills and principles to build God's Kingdom. Needs to be read by potential leaders as well as those in present leadership positions.

Bishop Richard Burruss, St. Louis, Missouri

It connects meaningfully with urban Christians from all ethnic backgrounds.

Pier McKenzie, President, Concerts of Prayer
of Greater New York

God will use your book to stretch the faith of those who read it.

Rick Ousley, The Church at Brook Hills, Birmingham, Alabama

Dr. Chand helps pastors and church leaders navigate the subtle waters of church leadership.

Edward Peecher, New Heritage Cathedral, Chicago, Illinois

This book will awaken the Spirit and challenge your intellect.

Wiley Jackson Jr., Word in Action Ministries, Atlanta, Georgia

He helps us chart our way through the future.

James Flanagan, Luther Rice Seminary, Lithonia, Georgia

Chand understands the times and knows what the church ought to do.

Philip M. Davis, Nations Ford Community Church,
Charlotte, North Carolina

This book will surely be a blessing to thousands . . . Chand's skills as an agent for visionary change are without equal.

Calvin W. Edwards, Calvin Edwards & Co., Atlanta, Georgia

››FUTURING

LEADING YOUR CHURCH INTO TOMORROW

SAMUEL R. CHAND | CECIL MURPHEY

HIGHLAND PARK, ILLINOIS

Published by Mall Publishing Company
641 Homewood Avenue
Highland Park, Illinois 60035
Toll Free: 1-877-203-2453
E-mail: info@mallpublishing.biz
Website: www.mallpublishing.biz

Printed in the United States of America

ISBN 0-9777273-8-6

For licensing / copyright information, for additional copies or for use in specialized settings contact:

Dr. Samuel R. Chand

950 Eagles Landing Parkway, Suite 295
Stockbridge, GA 30281
770-898-6464
www.samchand.com

To the most important person in my life,
my wife, Brenda,
who has been with me every step
and has been the major catalyst in my life.
—Sam Chand

For Shirley, with love—
Cec Murphey

Contents

Foreword

If there is to be a future church, today's church must change.

Dr. Chand is one of those rare leaders who has forged his way through many of the changes we now face. *Futuring: Leading Your Church into Tomorrow* has been skillfully written to equip us with the tools needed to press through change barriers.

For years we've upheld our church traditions and old ways of doing things. And yes, our traditions have given us the strong foundation on which we stand. Now, however, our charge is to be obedient to the Lord in carrying out his will—in a new day and in a new time. This requires us to be equipped mentally, physically, and spiritually with new tools that will help us get the job done. We can hold on to the good from the days of old, but it is critical that we forge ahead into the new—new presentations, new methods, new paradigms, and new mentalities that allow us to reach farther and spread the gospel more effectively than we did in the past.

Dr. Chand precisely sums up our mission as he writes that our foundational message must remain the same while our methods of presenting that message must change to meet the times and truly be effective.

Despite the obstacles, God needs Christians who are willing to walk in the vision he has given. Despite resistance, we must be willing to upgrade to new standards of excellence; despite opposition, we must abandon traditions that keep us separated from one another. We cannot be afraid to implement godly change for the good of the kingdom when God instructs us to confront the future.

This passion for frontline vision has placed Dr. Chand in the forefront of leadership training in America. God has used him to reach thousands with his teaching. With the same passion, he has clearly conveyed change principles that will keep us a step ahead.

Dr. Chand has helped us to see that we must go beyond the recognition of change to the actualization of change. If we grasp the truths contained in this book, we can become futuring leaders with futuring leadership traits for the futuring church. *Futuring: Leading Your Church into Tomorrow* is a lifeline for leaders everywhere in the body of Christ.

Bishop Eddie L. Long
Senior Pastor
New Birth Missionary Baptist Church
Lithonia, Georgia

Acknowledgments

*"Whenever you see a turtle sitting on top of a fence post,
you know the turtle didn't get there by itself!"*

author unknown

This turtle wants to acknowledge some of those who made this book possible.

- To my cowriter, Cecil ("Cec") Murphey, who has challenged me since I met him as my teacher at Beulah Heights Bible College in 1974.
- To my encourager and friend, Bishop Eddie L. Long, who is always future thinking.
- To John Maxwell, who gave me an opportunity of a lifetime to develop my leadership.
- To the Beulah Heights Bible College community, which gave me wings to fly high and roots to grow deep.
- To Jackie Armstrong, my executive assistant, who deals with all things marked "Sam."

- To Erick Moon, my special assistant, who makes life on the road so seamless.
- To Ron McManus, the first president of EQUIP, who gave me total autonomy.
- To John Hull, the current president of EQUIP, who has been my cheerleader and encourager.
- To my Christian business mentors who have taught me strategic and intentional living—Kevin Miller, Don Chapman, Billy Mitchell, John Weiland, Florida Ellis, Calvin Edwards, Steve Franklin, Bob Lupton, and many others.
- To my ministry mentors who have challenged me to greater godliness—Crawford Loritts, Oliver Haney, Roger Brumbalow, Mac McQuiston, Gerald Brooks, and an army of encouragers.
- To my daughters, Rachel and Deborah, who have taught me new paradigms as live-in faculty.
- And finally, to my life partner, Brenda, whose love and commitment keep challenges minimal and joys in overabundance.

Thank you!

Samuel R. Chand

ONE

This Ain't Your Daddy's Church

"This ain't your daddy's church!" said one pastor at a conference composed mostly of baby boomers. "The church of yesterday isn't the church of today."

Although that may sound obvious, churches tend to keep on doing things the way they did them a generation ago. Maybe we don't like to hear exhortations to reexamine our methods because we don't like being pushed to alter the way we've always done things.

Change has never been easy. In the late 1920s, many church leaders denounced the use of radio as a medium to present the gospel. Less than thirty years later, they debated the rightness of using television to proclaim the message. Such arguments sound ludicrous to emerging leaders of the future church.

We may not like certain innovations, but we can't get away from movement. If the past teaches us anything, it's that the methods we used a generation ago probably aren't effective now. For example, what we call "delivery systems" have continued to evolve—and that momentum won't stop with this generation. We started with e-mail and web access—almost unheard of in 1990—and now we order on-line and the Web Van delivers groceries to our home.

So where do we, the church, fit into this flux? Do we follow every whim or new idea? Of course not. But we don't stand rigidly firm either. The church is in the business of effectively and relevantly communicating a holistic, life-changing gospel; therefore, we have to adjust our methods to meet the times.

Here's the principle: Our foundational *message* remains the same. We stand on the fact that "Jesus Christ is the same yesterday and today and forever" (Heb. 13:8). Our *methods* for presenting the truth not only need to change; they must change.

As the man said: "This ain't your daddy's church!" And I would add, "It's not your granddaddy's either!" Too often church leaders have held on to old methods because they worked in the past with Daddy and Granddaddy. They may not work, however, with baby boomers, busters, and Gen-Xers, or mosaics—as we call the younger generations.

> Our *message* remains the same; our *methods* must change.

I've used the term *futurefaith* as my way of saying that we need to reexamine the "old-time religion." We need to separate methods and attitudes from biblical principles. Those of us who commit ourselves to grow and interact with the world around us realize that we need to change our thinking and our perceptions. What worked for Daddy and Granddaddy may be as obsolete as foot warmers in horse-drawn carriages.

Today change happens in the pulpit, in boardrooms, and on the streets. The catalysts are those I call "redefined leaders," people who hold leadership roles in the church. By that term, I refer to four significant characteristics: They (1) look at new paradigms of ministry; (2) are future focused; (3) embrace relevancy as a core issue; and (4) are vision-and-purpose driven. Leadership refers to the pastor surely but just as well to the office staff, Sunday school teachers, ushers, and anyone willing to work in the church.

In this book, my purpose is to

- encourage those in any position of leadership who want to communicate the gospel effectively
- show why and how we must change in the present to prepare for the years ahead
- suggest practical ways to enable us to develop into the future church—the church committed to the eternal gospel that seeks new methods to reach and enrich others
- serve as a catalyst for categories of new thinking

Then, Now, and in the Future*

Topic	Then—15 Years Ago	Now	Future—15 Years Out
The Leader	The single leader	The leadership team	Developing a community of leaders
Pastor/Leader Role	Primarily preaching	Leadership development and mobilizing the laity	Building the leadership team and distributing leadership throughout the organization

(continued)

*I am deeply indebted to Dr. Joe Samuel Ratliff Sr., pastor of Brentwood Baptist Church, Houston, Texas, for permitting me to copy this material.

Topic	Then—15 Years Ago	Now	Future—15 Years Out
Teaching Churches	Few in number and general in teaching	Several throughout the country both independent and denominationally affiliated	Many others in the future who will be more specialized in their expertise and teaching
Information	Desire for more information and it was *"pushed"* to the leader	It is *"pulled"* by the leader and customized to their needs or interests	Even more *"pulled,"* filtered and customized to specific needs *"That is exactly what I want"*
Outside Advice	There was a reluctance to ask for outside counsel and it was somewhat generalized	Leaders and churches are more open to outside counsel and it is specialized	Essential and will be customized for specific needs
Models of Ministry and Practice	Single models	Multiple models	Increased number of models and an interest in matching models to specific situations
External Consultants	*"Defined experts"* and usually involved an intervention	Specialized experts and more coaching and knowledge brokering	More interpretation, facilitating, mentoring and experience brokering
Failures	Hidden and not discussed	An openness to discussing and learning from them	More embracing and learning from them
Chief Resources	Money	Time	Knowledge, wisdom, and collaborative learning

TWO

The Futurefaith Church

What? Why? How? When?

Four questions loom before the church today—What? Why? How? and When?—and leaders have to answer each of them. Furthermore, they need to know which one to answer first and in what order to answer the others. Too many church leaders respond to the wrong questions and in the wrong order. In so doing, they come up with ineffective answers.

Effective leaders know that two of the four questions take priority. The question leaders choose to answer first tells us much about their attitudes and methods.

In this book, I use the term *futuring leaders* to refer to church leaders who have a firm vision of where they want to go in the future. Consequently, futuring leaders first answer What? Then they ask Why?

By answering these two questions first, they begin to define the direction in which the local congregation should go and to form a process to get them headed in that direction. Since their search for answers has a direct relationship to the mission and vision of the institution, they need to define their problem areas. The question *What?* does exactly that.

"What is the challenge before us?" futuring leaders must first ask. Their question may take various forms, but it will lead them to ask and answer others. Once they discover the solution, they will seek options to implement the *what.*

Once they have decided on *what,* they are ready to move on to the second question: Why? They need to understand the reason they are taking a particular step. Thus they ask, "Why are we doing this?"

When I asked one pastor why his congregation had chosen to underwrite a particular program, he stared at me for several seconds.

"Everyone knows why," he said. "The answer is obvious even to people who don't know the message of salvation." He spoke to me as if I were a child.

I just smiled. But what if I had answered, "I don't know why." Would he have explained? Or would he have sneered at my stupidity?

Or wasn't I really stupid?

This leads me to ask, Do we have the right to assume that *everyone* in our church knows why leadership chooses to do a certain thing? I doubt it.

In my roles as president of Beulah Heights Bible College (BHBC) and Urban Leadership Development, as well as conference speaker for EQUIP, I visit more than eighty churches a year and speak to a quarter-million leaders from nearly fifty denominations. My conclusion is that, unless prompted otherwise, most leaders don't take time to organize their thoughts around *why.* Even when they do, they respond only from their immediate and localized perspective. They assume the way they think is the way every committed Christian thinks.

Predictable Times of Conflict in Churches

1. Special days such as Christmas and Easter; special events such as weddings, funerals, and celebrations, as well as family and singles activities.
2. Fund-raising and budget time.
3. When adding new staff. Adding new staff members not only means there will be changes in relationships and procedures, but also the congregation will see changes in direction and priorities.
4. Change in leadership styles. Whenever new leaders emerge, things don't remain the way they were before. This also happens whenever the present leadership modifies or alters its style. Leadership shifts occur in every phase of the life of the congregation from the ushering program to youth activities.
5. The pastor's vacation. When the pastor is gone, who is in charge? Who makes decisions? This is a time when power struggles easily erupt.
6. Changes in the pastor's family. This may mean the pastor's marriage, divorce, remarriage, the birth of a child, or the death of a spouse or child.
7. Rising leadership. Baby boomers (born between 1946 and 1964) moved into leadership roles within the church in their thirties. Their leadership is being challenged just as they themselves challenged the seniors and builders (the previous generations). Each generation lives a significantly different lifestyle and holds differing values.

For instance, the pastor makes a big push for increased evangelism. From his perspective some of the answers to *why* would be:

- We can win more people to Jesus Christ.
- We'll have more people in the church.

- We'll have more money to expand our church programs.
- We'll have a greater influence in the community.

His list of *why* answers may not be the same as that of the congregation he's trying to lead.

By thinking of others' reasons, fears, and needs, futuring leaders can understand the resistance and either rethink their own purposes or find ways to get into others' frames of reference. They also avoid inevitable conflict because they have already prepared for and overcome most of the hindrances.

Here's an example of how I confronted *why* at Beulah Heights Bible College. In 1999 we first wrestled with a *what* question. As president I wanted to offer an undergraduate curriculum and degree taught totally in a language other than English. My *what* began with this question: What constituency—what people whose primary language is not English—already exists and wants us to provide training? I had no group in mind but was concerned that although the United States has become a pluralistic society, most of our outreach is only to those who are like us—that is, to those who speak English. I couldn't get away from the burden to reach out to people of a different culture and language. For several weeks I pondered the question, discussed it with staff members, and talked to friends. The burden wouldn't go away.

After serious exploration and study among the staff, we decided that the people to focus on were Brazilians, whose language is Portuguese.

Now we faced the second question, and I gave the following answers.

Why do we want to do this? Since its beginnings in the early 1900s, the mission of BHBC has been to reach and equip unreached groups to teach their own people.

Why? Second-language groups are increasing in number in the United States. Because of language barriers, they often don't get the education they need to go to their own people and teach them the gospel.

Why? The Brazilians represent another "market."

Why? The concept of missions has changed and is no longer limited to American churches sending missionaries to foreign lands. It now also includes missionaries coming to this land and working among their own people. There are more foreign-born missionaries in America today than there are missionaries from America in other countries.

Why? If we train the Brazilians in their own language and with an understanding of their culture, they can go back to their country as leaders and teachers. Furthermore,

- They won't have to apply for visas.
- They already speak the language and don't have to learn it or work with interpreters.
- They have natural bridges to their own culture.
- Their credibility is already in place because they are of the same race and nationality.

After a lengthy study of answering those two significant questions, in the fall of 2000, BHBC started a second-language group in Portuguese, and twenty-three students enrolled. The following year we had thirty-three enrolled.

I have presented you the *why* answer in several different ways. However, I have given these from my point of view as the leader and president of BHBC. That is the mistake leaders often make. They are already sold on what they want to do; consequently, they move immediately into implementing their new concepts. Thus, such ideas often become the leaders' projects to push (or impose!) on others who are involved in serving and carrying out the *what*. This helps to explain the resistance—active and passive—many leaders encounter.

Before I could go any further in starting a second-language curriculum at BHBC, I needed to focus on the people who would stand behind the program and make it work—those who work in the admissions office, the registrar's office, the dean's office, and the faculty, custodians, and groundskeepers. I wanted everyone within the BHBC structure to know the *why* from his or her individual level.

In addition to some of the statements I made above—and they weren't exclusive to my perspective—I gathered comments from the people who would do most of the work if we began such a program. They said:

- "This will mean more work."
- "You will face more challenges."
- "Why can't we leave things the way they are?"
- "Why meddle with success? After all, the school is in the best shape it's ever been in."

Those of us on the decision-making end tried to listen carefully to staff members' resistance and then answer their questions without imposing our ideas on them. We tried to give direct and honest answers.

During the process, I told them, "All of us want to multiply ourselves. That is, we want to leave a legacy on this earth after we're gone. In one sense, such actions immortalize us and make us bigger than ourselves, thus spreading our influence. We want to do something to leave an afterglow after our glow is gone."

My intention wasn't to wear down the staff members or force them to agree. I wanted them to look at this situation from every possible perspective. I also promised to listen and evaluate any objections they offered.

"With this new curriculum we are becoming a part of history," I said. "This is something entirely new, not only to BHBC, but also to Bible school curricula everywhere. Right here in Atlanta we're going to leave behind a powerful legacy. The students we teach will influence people all over the country of Brazil. They will be able to because each of us plays a role in equipping them."

No one seemed intimidated by my enthusiasm or my vision even though several staff members raised legitimate concerns. Wisely, they evaluated the new program from their individual perspectives and considered how the changes would affect them personally.

By the end of our meeting, we had reached the consensus to go ahead.

Once leaders have asked and answered What? and Why? they're ready to move on to the next two questions: How? and When? This second set of questions implies action. It's as if we're saying, "We've made the decision to act. Now we need to figure out how to go about accomplishing our goal and determine when we can implement our plan."

Again, here is where many leaders miss out. They need to be aware that implementing the *how* and *when* means change. I like to think of it this way: If we think differently, we'll see differently. How we think shapes the actions we choose.

The greatest challenge facing church leaders is making executive decisions from a variety of different viewpoints. Sometimes we make decisions from the perspective of management or maintenance. At other times we have operated from a fix-it point of view. Rarely have we pulled in all those who will be involved by the changes and said, "You are part of this change in procedure. Your job may be to answer the telephone, but even that is a vital ingredient in this program."

I understood this clearly one morning when I was driving to work. I was listening to an AM radio station on the first day of the new school year. The news anchor was interviewing an official from Gwinett County, a suburban area north of Atlanta, and they were discussing the fact that the county had become the state's fastest growing area. Referring primarily to the building of new schools, the interviewer asked, "How do you keep up with that growth?"

The official replied, "This process started years ahead of today. We began to study the demographics and get building permits and take bids. We decided on the need for natural gas, water, and electricity, and we spoke with all the providers. We examined the job market, checked migration trends, and began to project the number of people who would move to our county. Then we considered financing—bond referendum, tax increase, and other ways to raise revenue."

For possibly two minutes the man spoke of the structure and the personnel they would need once they began to build. Then he talked about how they would have to coordinate everything with the already existing school system. "So you see, it takes three to four years' planning before we ever open the first new school doors."

"Yes!" I shouted to the radio. "That's the way to do it!"

Christian organizations do little of that type of planning. It's almost as if they say, "We need to move into that new growing area. Let's buy land, build a big building, and open our doors at eleven o'clock on a Sunday morning. People will come, and once they come, we'll learn who's in our community."

That's a parody, of course, but it means that those with such an attitude aren't actively reaching out into the community or asking, "What's going to be happening four years down the road? How can we prepare today for tomorrow?"

Here's another way to look at the same issue. Let's compare the difference between old leadership styles and new leadership styles, or furturefaith thinking. In the old style—and I refer primarily to the methods used prior to the end of the twentieth century—leaders studied the past and understood the way things operated in 1959 or 1989. When they moved into 2000, they made a few changes—that is, they adapted to what was going on—but mainly they replicated what they and others had done in the past. Because they made a few adaptations, they called that progress.

"What did they do *back then?*" was the primary question used to help them cope in the *present.*

In contrast to the old style, the new leadership peers into the future, pauses, thinks about the present, and asks:

- What's going to happen in the future?
- How can we position ourselves in the present to be ready to move into the future?
- How can we design a program for what lies ahead?

Futurefaith leaders get their answers by looking at such factors as demographics and economic growth the way the officials of Gwinett County did. They use those answers to shape the present and guide them toward the future.

For example, most Americans already know that the largest minority population in the United States is Hispanic. That means we need to do more training of people in the business world to be able to deal with the Hispanic culture and language. Some of our school systems, long aware of this, have already begun to offer Spanish in elementary grades. They looked at the future and then figured out how to make the present fit and flow into that picture.

Preserving the Past or Shaping the Future?

Too often, however, church leaders still caught up in preserving the attitudes and traditions that prevailed thirty years ago don't know how to look at the future. For too long, those in every level of leadership have taken a reactive posture, resulting in attitudes and vision usually lagging about ten years behind industry and technology. Church leaders could move ahead by simply asking: "As a local congregation and as witnesses of Jesus Christ, *what* are our needs? *What* are the needs we see around us that we can help to meet? *What* kinds of needs will we need to meet in the years ahead?"

As we form answers, we need to remind ourselves that most church members live in a highly technological world six days a week. My cowriter, Cecil Murphey, has his own web site, which he started in 1999. He told me that in 1996 it never would have occurred to him to consider such a thing. Even in 1997, how many people would have envisioned having their own web site? Yet today numerous congregations have their own web sites.

Many people attend a church where song lyrics are displayed on a screen by an overhead projector. Those who sit near the back squint, and if the light isn't right, they can't read the words. They have been using that system for a decade, and it's already out of date. When I preach in larger, forward-looking churches, they have huge screens the size of a wall on either side of the platform on which they project lyrics and often the music. They also project the speaker on those screens so that he or she can be viewed from anywhere in the building.

> Moore's Law, developed by Gordon Moore of Intel, predicted that every eighteen months to two years, the power and speed of computer chips will double.

The sound system microphone used to hang from the ceiling with a long cord just above the pulpit. In progressive churches, microphones are dispersed all over the congregation. The hearing impaired have their own wireless systems and don't have to be hooked into the first three pews. Now they can sit anywhere they want.

Some churches have "seeded" singers with cordless microphones. When the congregation sings, those seeded singers encourage those sitting around them to sing out. As a result, the singing has a more vigorous, exciting sound.

Some churches think they're progressive because they have finally purchased a fax machine. They're still sharing the telephone line with the fax machine and seem scarcely aware that multifunction scanner/fax machines are rapidly making single-function devices relics. Many churches are finally starting to use e-mail and voice mail to respond to incoming telephone calls. In short, technology needs to hit every area of every church if we're going to keep up with the future of this society. We need it in our sanctuaries, classrooms, parking lots, and offices.

Futurefaith leaders should know this: We need to use technology.

I like to think of the present situation in the church as being much like the use of a remote control. These days most families have that little battery-operated mechanism for running TV, VCR, CD, and DVD players. People have become so accustomed to remotes that even when they leave home, they take mental remotes with them. They're still using those remotes even when they attend church. They stare at the strange building that doesn't look like anything except a church. It has stained-glass windows on the outside, perhaps a bell, and certainly a steeple. Suddenly and unconsciously, "click-click" goes the remote, and they say to themselves, "How does this relate to me? Why should I listen? Is this real life?"

Perhaps they do come inside and sit in a pew—an uncomfortable piece of furniture used nowhere else today except in church buildings. They sit down and listen to pastors who preach the same sermons in content and length that they preached ten years ago.

"This is the answer!" the preachers cry out. "This is the way to____ [salvation, growth, healing, prosperity, or peace]." They have a number of specific answers to handle each problem that confronts the local congregation, the church at large, and society in general. Unfortunately for those preachers, they haven't figured out that some of those problems aren't so answerable and directions aren't as clear as they once were.

"Click-click" and the remote switches to another mental channel.

From the Absolute to the Ambiguous

We have moved from a world of the absolute to the ambiguous. We're asking ethical questions that people haven't asked before; for example:

- Fifty years ago, how many committed Christians married outside their denomination? Who worries about that today?
- Twenty years ago, how many churches acknowledged that some marriages between believers didn't last until parted by death?
- In Mama's church, how many members seriously debated issues such as euthanasia or sexual reassignment?
- A generation ago, how many Christians expressed concern about the environment, practiced recycling, or questioned whether we would have enough fossil fuels for our grandchildren's generation?
- When I was a boy, I heard Christians scream out against cremation, but who fights that issue today?

Futurefaith leaders have moved from answering questions that nobody asks anymore to discussing the nitty-gritty issues of life that concern and confuse people.

Society has changed; we have lost the stability our parents and grandparents enjoyed and took for granted. For instance, numerous studies indicate that most people with college degrees aren't working in the field of their educational major. In the past, people went to work for a company, stayed with them for the next forty years, and retired with a watch and a good-bye party. Who is engaged in that kind of long-term employment now? One researcher estimates that most people in this century will hold at least seven different jobs. The editors of *The New Millennial* (September 2001) project that those who enter the job market after 2010 will change jobs every year.

What does this mean for futurefaith leaders and for congregations that yearn to forge ahead? They begin to think like futurefaith leaders when they recognize that people live in constant transition and that, despite

> Futuring leaders ask What? and Why? before they consider How? and When?
>
> The style and format of worship services were patterned after practices of a century ago. Those methods no longer attract people to the faith.

all the technology and convenience, basic human needs have not changed.

People still hurt. They need to know they are loved and especially that God loves them and wants their fellowship. Futuring Sunday school teachers no longer focus on what David did with the four unused stones when he killed Goliath. Instead, they teach about the role of prayer in coping with stress or how to have inner peace when the company downsizes.

Futuring pastors no longer preach forty-five-minute sermons, because they know the remotes are clicking away, and they would be tuned out before they had preached even thirty minutes. In fact, maybe sermons need to be done in snippets—points interspersed with songs, Bible readings, dramas, and video clips. Someone said we need to think of the modern sermon as "Karaoke preaching," in which the preacher stands in the middle of the congregation like an interactive television talk show host.

The futuring church must find new ways of presenting the gospel before they're tuned out by the ever-present mental remotes.

Thinking in New Ways

To move into the futurefaith mentality, we have to accept one important reality: Most worship services are patterned after practices of a century ago, and those methods no longer attract people to the faith.

Futuring leaders must move into a thinking-leading style of leadership in which they see relationships and possibilities that still elude others. This is the idea I had in mind once when I spoke to a group of pastors at Beulah Heights. "The greatest challenge is not your location. It is not your finances, and it is not your staff," I said. "The greatest challenge is your thinking. If you can change your way of thinking, you can change everything."

I reminded them that we're in a thinking era and we have to question everything. In the past, we continued to do things a certain way because that was the way the leaders before us operated. That plan no longer works. Futuring leaders question everything.

- "Why are we doing this?"
- "Are we still doing that?"
- "Is that the best way to use our resources?"
- "Is there a better way to do this?"
- "Why is she still doing that?"
- "Is he competent to do this?"

Here is an illustration of new thinking. In early 2001, we started thinking of what it would be like if we offered early-morning classes at BHBC—classes that started at 6:30 A.M. The thinking behind this idea came about because several of us realized that many of our students could only attend classes at night after they had finished work. Often they were mentally drained and physically tired.

What would it be like, we asked, if we offered classes for people who wanted to study for an hour every morning before they went to work? That way, after they finished at their workplaces, they could go home and be with their families rather than hassle with childcare issues and getting food on the table before they rushed off to class.

"This is really new and radical thinking," someone said. "Let's try it."

We had no guarantees. We didn't know if even one student would sign up. Nevertheless, our staff stood behind the idea, and we worked with the paradigm. In the fall of 2001, we began to offer early-morning classes. More than sixty students enrolled.

We had made the right decision. By changing our thinking and looking at our options, we met needs that others had paid no attention to.

In 2001 the U.S. Census Bureau released a study to show how many years it took before 60 percent of households used the various media technologies. Here are the results:

1. Telephone	30 years
2. Radio	10 years
3. Television	5 years
4. Cable TV	27 years
5. VCRs	10 years
6. Computers	15 years
7. Internet	2 years

The study also indicated the following:

- in 2000, 45 percent of children under age eighteen are connected to the Internet. (That's more than 30 million children.)
- on any given day, 58 million Americans logged on—an increase of 9 million from July to December 2000.
- in the last half of 2000, 20 million more people had used the Internet to pursue their hobbies and 14 million more had used it to buy products than in the first half of 2000.
- there was a sharp increase in the number of middle-aged, African American, and Hispanic Internet users during the second half of 2000.
- by the end of 2000 when elections were big news items, 17 percent of Internet users received their news and information on-line—double the number who were getting such news on a typical day in October 2000.

THREE

Immigrants vs. Natives

An unaccredited story that has been making the rounds on e-mail illustrates the importance of new leadership thinking.

In an ancient time in the city of Rome, a number of Romans became perturbed because of the increasing number of Jews who had moved into the city. "Soon they'll outnumber us and take over," they cried.

Emissaries appealed to the pope. "There are too many Jews. We must get rid of them." They insisted that the pope decree that all Jews leave, and they would have exactly three days to get out.

Obviously, when the Jews heard about this contemplated action, they appealed to His Holiness. They got an audience with the pope and argued for their being able to stay. After an hour of negotiation, the pope and the Jewish leaders decided to settle the matter with a theological debate in St. Peter's Square. If the Jews won the debate, they could remain. If not, they would leave.

The agreement had only one catch—neither side could speak. Everything had to be done silently.

By the appointed day, builders had erected a large platform at St. Peter's Square. The pope sat on one side surrounded by his cardinals. On the other side sat a Jew named Moshe with half a dozen rabbinical leaders.

When the debate began, the pope raised his right index finger and circled the sky. Moshe stared at him, nodded, and with his index finger, pointed toward the earth.

After several minutes of silent contemplation, the pope held up three fingers, and Moshe held up his right index finger and shook it at the prelate.

Silence prevailed for quite a time, and finally the pope pulled out the Eucharist (Lord's Supper) and offered it to his cardinals. Moshe stared, shrugged, and pulled an apple from his pocket and began to munch on it.

A perspiring, frustrated pope stood and said, "You are too good! The Jews may stay!" He and his entourage left.

After the Jews finished celebrating and shouting, the cardinals surrounded the pope. "What went on?" they asked. "We did not understand the debate."

"As you know, I lifted my index finger and circled it in the air," he explained. "When I did that, I was saying that God is all around us. He reminded me that God is right here as well.

"I then held up the three fingers to remind him that we believe in God the Father, God the Son, and God the Holy Spirit. But he raised one finger and said, 'Don't we all believe in the same God?' Then I pulled out the Eucharist to remind him of the sacrificial and atoning death of our Lord and Savior, Jesus Christ. He in turn pulled out the apple to remind us of how sin got started in the world."

Meanwhile, on the other side of town, the rabbis asked, "Moshe, what happened?"

He replied, "When the pope lifted up his index finger and circled the sky and said, 'I'm going to clear Rome of all you Jews,' I pointed my finger down and said, 'We're staying right here.' When he lifted three fingers saying, 'You have three days to leave,' I lifted one finger to say, 'Not one of us is leaving.'"

"So, what happened at the end?"

"Oh, that. He took out his lunch, and I pulled out mine."

The point of this story is that we send messages that we assume are clear and unmistakable. Those who receive messages sometimes end up with a different interpretation.

Two Groups

That's where we are at this time. In the pulpits, Sunday school classrooms, and every area of church leadership, we make pronouncements as the pope did—and we often do it with authority. We have historical precedent behind us, we know what we're saying and doing, and we know why. What we don't grasp is that those who receive our messages have a different outlook and divergent values, and the message we send isn't the message they receive.

One way to understand this dilemma is to talk about the two distinct groups of people in almost every congregation—immigrants and natives (terms I borrowed from Leonard Sweet). As you read this, ask yourself, "Am I an immigrant or a native?" If you'll seriously consider the question and its implications, the answer may surprise you. Neither is bad.

Natives, as the term implies, are those who have been in the church—especially in one particular congregation—for a long time. They have been there long enough to know the congregation's history and can speak of the trials and hardships of building the membership through the years. Someone has said that everyone who is forty years old and has been in a church for at least a decade is a native. That age isn't meant literally, but is used only to refer to the general thinking of those in that group. I know some seventy-eight-year-olds who still think young. I also know twenty-five-year-olds who are native in their thinking.

Immigrants, by contrast, come into a church and try to understand the language of a congregation, which is often like a foreign dialect to them. To fit in, they have to tread carefully until they learn the sacred words and symbols. Only then will they be accepted as orthodox believers.

The two groups can be distinguished by contrasting their characteristics.

Natives	Immigrants
Slow deciders	Fast deciders
Threatened by change	Lead change
"Yes . . . but"	"Yes . . . and"
Linear thinking	Looped thinking
Fight against chaos and instability	Can live with chaos, uncertainty, and instability
Learn formally	Learn by discovery—by doing it
Visual—primarily through books	Visual—primarily through TV and media

In some ways, of course, all of us are immigrants even if we are natives within our local church. For example, helping my two daughters with their homework overwhelms me. I can't sit down in the evening and assist them with their math homework the way my parents did with me. In my day, we learned fractions and decimals by a different process than students arrive at them now. Not that one is right and the other is wrong; they simply do their math from another perspective. Consequently, in this case, they're immigrants and I'm a native.

To carry this further, when I did homework at home, we had no interference from the radio, TV, tape player, or CD player. We sat at the kitchen table before or after dinner and worked there until we completed our assignments.

Both my daughters amaze me. They can have the TV blaring, talk with a friend on the phone, and type an e-mail message—all while they're doing homework. Their generation is made up of multitaskers while their parents were taught to be one-task people.

Here are a few other contrasts:

- My generation was into permanence and stability, but that's not possible or desirable today.
- We readily accepted whatever authority figures said, but today's youth question authority. They raise eyebrows at authoritative voices or react cynically to once-accepted messages.
- Print was the truth medium. If we read something in a newspaper, and especially if it appeared in book form, it was truth without question. For today's youth, TV is the truth—well, usually.
- When I asked, "Why?" my father would answer, "Just because I said so," and that would end the discussion. That's not the end of the discussion now. In fact, we rarely speak those words to our children.

How does this relate to an organization such as the church? Let's say the pastor is an immigrant—which is likely when first coming to a new congregation. Who greets the immigrant? The natives, of course—and that includes the staff as well as the congregation. How the pastor and natives communicate with one another becomes extremely important. (Of course, some pastors are natives—they may have moved two or three times in their career, but they take the past with them and replicate what they have taught and preached for the previous twenty years.)

Natives are those who perpetuate the past by trying to relive it in the present. Whatever they are doing now or have been doing is the "right thing." This often means that when immigrants attend a church, the teaching natives prescribe books and courses written by natives who learned from other natives.

Immigrants come into the church and hear the same kind of sermons their parents heard in 1975. The church service is still predictable. After they have attended two Sundays, they know how the service will start and when it is going to end. They know what will happen at 11:15 and can guess within sixty seconds when the service will end.

Today many pastors come in as natives—bringing the past with them—and they hire staff members who are mostly immigrants. The new staff people are younger, have been to college since the pastor graduated, and are reading and listening to different things.

In most cases, the congregation—if the church is growing—is composed of natives and an increasing number of immigrants. The immigrants differ from their parents, all the structure is different, and the leadership is still native—in its thinking, attitude, and ways of doing things.

When I start asking natives the *why* question, they sometimes resent the question itself or act offended as though the query is a criticism. To an immigrant, *why* is a reasonable thing to ask, because he or she has been taught to raise issues. Immigrants are a questioning people; natives were taught to be an answering people.

What does this mean for the people who want to bring in the immigrants? For one thing, unlike the generation before them, they face the reality that those immigrants aren't searching for leaders who have all the answers. Rather, they seek leaders who raise relevant questions. The most effective leaders sit in a business meeting and ask, "What about____?" Those leaders know that if they raise the right issues, they can help guide others to the right answers. They don't have to provide all the knowledge, insight, and wisdom, but they do have to point the way.

> The future is not the result of choices among alternative paths offered in the present. It is a place created—created first in the mind and the will; created next in activity.
>
> Walt Disney

Activity used to drive our thinking and our ministry. For instance, a Sunday school superintendent would say, "We're going to have backyard Bible clubs all summer." That's an activity, and the clubs were effective—in 1980.

That style of thinking has changed. Today if a native says, "We're going to have a backyard Bible club," an immigrant immediately asks, "Why do we want to do that?"

A flustered native sees this questioning as opposition or resistance.

The immigrant might then say, "Okay, but why the Smith backyard? Why not at the Hansons across the street or the Randolphs in the next block? What's so strategic about the Smith backyard?"

After the native reluctantly gives an answer, another immigrant asks, "What are we going to do with the clubs to follow up?"

Twenty years ago, some natives hadn't ever considered anything beyond holding the club activities, presenting Jesus Christ as the Savior, and informing the congregation of the number of first-time decisions for

Jesus Christ. For them, just having and staffing a back-yard Bible study was an event. They did their service for the Lord and didn't look ahead.

Today's leaders are saying, "We can no longer be an event-oriented society; we need to move to being a process-driven society." An event is the means and end combined into one. That is, an event begins and ends, while a process focuses primarily on the means, recognizing that the end is usually a mirage. For immigrants, there is only process and no ultimate end in sight. An immigrant is comfortable with the process, whereas natives tend to feel anxious.

Immigrants, for example, think like this. Someone asks, "Why don't we establish places of worship outside the traditional church building?" Actually, this change is already taking place, and it came about because futuring leaders recognized needs, and then they asked and answered the right questions. From there they began activities to respond to those needs.

As a result, some organizations now provide chapels or places of worship at their work sites. Many churches use movie theaters and hotels. Business gurus like Stephen Covey and Ken Blanchard recommend them. Even some airports now have chapels and paid chaplains.

From Transaction to Transformation

Immigrants understand that people have needs at pressure points in their lives. They're trying to meet those needs through collaboration and connections rather than depending on one or two churches that try to do everything themselves. It's a matter of cooperating instead of lone-wolfing.

This leads us to another serious question for futuring leaders. They ask, "Who else do I need to make this happen?" If futurefaith leaders strive to find the answer, things not only begin to happen, but immigrants feel that the natives care about them.

No longer can a church say, "Here we are! Come and find out what we believe." Now the futuring churches are asking, "How can we help?" Instead of saying, "There are many homeless, so let's start a new homeless shelter," they're asking, "Why should we start that ministry when there's already a shelter downtown? How can we resource them?" And they're asking, "Why should we start a home for unwed mothers? Let's find out who is already providing that service and then figure out what we can do to enhance their efforts." Or "Why should we clog up our basement with musty clothes when there are places we can take them?"

> For churches to grow, the natives have to adapt to the immigrants' language and needs rather than forcing immigrants to make changes to fit in.

The question is not "What can *we* do?" The question is "What can we do through others?" That's a new way of thinking. Rather than asking, "How can I increase my power and influence? How can I enlarge my kingdom?" we should ask, "How can I empower somebody else and still meet my mission?" This kind of thinking is transformational and not just transactional. Transformation happens when there is active collaboration toward the same goals, and then the mission becomes a win-win proposition.

When people move from transaction to transformation, they're reaching into immigrant country. Instead of trying to do everything themselves, they're learning to empower others. Such transformation begins with a readiness to change.

FOUR

Change Readiness

Beginning with *change readiness,* the following chapters describe the ten traits of futuring leadership. *Change readiness* describes the attitude of embracing rather than resisting change. Whenever change comes about, many leaders focus positively on the gains and overlook the fact that many people concentrate on loss. We need to learn to handle both. It is difficult for natives to accept change because they perceive it as giving up.

Those who want to be a vital part of the futuring church must ask themselves two questions:

First, what in *my* thinking needs to change?
Second, what keeps *me* from making those changes?

I regularly ask myself these two questions, and the answers I get aren't always pleasant. In my case, I have to loosen the screws. That is, I have to let go of more things, delegate, and surrender control.

The Ten Traits of Futuring Leadership

1. Change Readiness
2. Expecting the Unexpected
3. Sensitive Issues
4. Communication Today
5. Technophilia vs. Technophobia
6. Healthy Lifestyles
7. Lifelong Learning
8. Creative Leadership
9. Timing
10. Future Gazing

As a native and a church leader, I was taught (indirectly) that leaders are always in control. I came to this quite naturally, because my father was a pastor and I became a pastor. And because I loved and respected my father, I emulated him in many ways.

Like other pastors who went through ministerial training when I did, my tendency was to become a control freak. We hate the term, but it's a strong part of most leaders. Although we never admitted to having a need to control or dominate, the need was nonetheless real. Whether consciously or subconsciously, we believed we were the center of the church universe. It was our responsibility to keep everything moving in the "right direction" (translate "right direction" as *my* way of doing things). If we didn't keep everything within our control, we had failed!

When I became president of Beulah Heights Bible College, I transferred that need for control and taking charge. I didn't enlarge my understanding, and I didn't change tactics or attempt new strategies. I went from being a pastor to a college president, but my operating methods stayed the same. That is, they did until I began asking myself those two questions—and demanding answers from myself.

My Answers

The answers I had to admit to myself came out of much heart searching, deep introspection, and not a small amount of embarrassment.

First, "What in my thinking needs to change?" I needed to realize that I don't have to control every action and every outcome. This isn't a question we answer once and it's over. It's a question that demands frequent internal checkups.

Second, "What keeps me from making those changes?" Sam Chand was the biggest problem, because he didn't change quickly. He understood the principle of future-faith leadership for several years before he began to learn to live by the principle of surrendering control (a stronger and perhaps more accurate way of saying it is "giving up power"). I still have a little trouble with him in that area, but he is learning.

Most of us have an operating principle we live by, especially when we are thrust into leadership roles. Twenty years ago, we referred to that as our *model,* and today we use the word *paradigm.* However we say it, we mean that each of us has a set of internal values and attitudes that determines how we function. My paradigm was that the pastor is in *total* control and holds the power in the church. Many of us natives grew up with that same model. At its extreme, it means that no one dares to make a single decision unless it bears the pastor's imprint. The pastor becomes the deciding factor and final word on everything that happens in the church.

Part of my growth in the futuring church has been learning to trust others—and it has been a learning process—and encouraging them to express their abilities. At one point, I would have said "allowing them" to express their abilities, indicating that I still held control and was to be viewed as the permission giver. Then I learned that the best use of power is to empower others.

We can't fully make the ten traits of futuring church leadership, discussed in the following chapters, realities until we probe deep within ourselves and ask the two questions with which I started this chapter. So before you read on, ask yourself, "Am *I* ready to change?"

Preparing for Change

Change readiness means we're prepared to embrace change rather than resist it—ready to think new thoughts, adjust our attitudes, and be open to whatever lies ahead of us. It's a mental thing and a spiritual decision. It's also easier to talk about than to make a reality.

We need to remind ourselves that when we alter our attitudes we can produce vast gains. That's the primary reason we advocate change—we readily see the benefits of our decisions. If we [name the activity], then we will [grow, mature, witness more effectively].

We tend to see only the sunshine up ahead and put the "gain spin" on innovative ideas. But change has another side—it also brings about loss. Too often those in leadership don't pause to consider that aspect. Furthermore, those who have to adjust are often ignored. They are the ones who must make the change, which they didn't originate, and they respond in terms of loss. They may say things such as,

- "It won't be the same around here."
- "I used to know everyone by name."
- "I'll feel lost by the sheer size of the building."

- "I liked the music we used to have. Why do we have to keep adding songs that nobody can sing?" (Note that "nobody" refers to those with the same attitudes.)
- "What's wrong with the way we used to do it?"

What these people are really asking is "What do I have to give up?" and "Why do I have to give in? Why can't others give in?"

If they think in such categories and if the losses are too large, leaders will encounter resistance, quiet acquiescence, subtle sabotage, or open rebellion.

Let's go back to the Brazilian extension courses. What I presented to everyone on the staff was gain, because that is how I saw the situation. Gain for us was that we would be reaching our mission. Jesus commanded us, "Go and make disciples of all nations, baptizing them in the name of the Father and of the Son and of the Holy Spirit, and teaching them to obey everything I have commanded you" (Matt. 28:19–20).

I believed we would be following that command in a more strategic way than we had been doing previously. But because I assumed the staff would view my ideas differently, I met with them so that we could consider it together.

As I had expected, they expressed loss. These are typical of their comments:

- "What will this do to our computer system?"
- "This will make more work for us, and we're already working at full capacity."
- "What if we don't understand the Brazilians?"
- "How are we going to control the Portuguese-speaking faculty when we don't know what they're

teaching? They may be bringing in false doctrine, and how will we know?"

As I responded to their concerns, I began to think of my basic philosophy. That is, some people see a half-full glass while others see a half-empty one, and it's not really a matter of optimists versus pessimists; it's just how people are. How people view a change issue also depends on how leaders frame the questions. Their response reflects the leaders' change readiness and willingness to promote and thus lead change. Mutual trust is vital to the process.

I approached the Beulah Heights staff about incorporating a Brazilian curriculum by saying, "Try to rewind your mental VCR and return to the last board meeting. Think about how much time we spent in that meeting on what had already happened and how little time we spent on what would happen."

They agreed that we spend enormous amounts of time discussing what happened last week, last month, or last year.

In typical church meetings, the leaders talk extensively about what they need to be doing now, but they tend to spend little time discussing what the future holds for them and their congregation's ministry. They talk even less about the implications of change for those who hold leadership positions. Asking, "What needs to happen?" is not as important as asking, "As leaders, what do we need to do?"

Those of us in leadership positions—any leadership position in the church—need to ask, "What am I doing that prevents our ministry from going forward?"

We may not like the answers, but we need to hear them anyway. As leaders in any area of ministry, we need to challenge the other members of our committees and boards to consider the future and to be open to change.

One way to go about that is to urge them to reserve in every meeting an agenda item that focuses on the future.

"We need to do this in every meeting," we can say as we reserve a place for discussion. We might also prompt dialogue by asking, "What would you like to see happen? What changes would you like to make as we face our future?"

I try to remind people of the world outside our church doors. Think of it this way. Today as I drive down the highway, I see a huge sign indicating that there is a Kroger store to my right. Tomorrow it may not be there. On the third day, a new grocery chain may have moved in. Things change—we all know that. What we haven't fully grasped, however, is how rapidly they change.

> Did you know? One hundred years ago, 75 percent of the population worked on farms.

Even if we endorse or approve a plan for a new form of ministry, that's not the end. As leaders at every level in the church, we need to ask ourselves, "What is going on with us—individually and as a congregation—that will stop this form of ministry from going forward?"

Sometimes when I make such suggestions, people stare back at me, hardly understanding what I'm trying to say. So usually I give them an example, such as this: Let's say a church is structured so that there are seven elders. What would it be like if each elder had a responsibility to do research as part of that leadership position? One researches the socioeconomic demographics of the community. A second studies the ethnic issues, problems, and opportunities within the community. A third focuses on environmental issues and what the congregation can do to take care of the earth God has given us—especially the part around the church and neighborhood. A fourth investigates the learning and teaching styles in the area schools and explains to Sunday school teachers how they might use those styles to enhance their ministry.

If each of the seven has a research assignment and brings back a report, the church will have some indication of what the future will look like. The church may need to bring in a consultant to pull all the information together and then begin to plan for that future.

Let's say this congregation focuses on the next three years. If they study what is going on now and use the benefit of their research to project what lies ahead, they will function as a futuring church.

For instance, instead of declaring, "This is now a transitional community," they won't have to think in that kind of category, for they would have known three years earlier that it was going to become transitional and change from single housing to apartment housing or that the area was changing from a residential community to a commercial neighborhood. My point is that a futuring church would have acknowledged the transition before it became readily apparent to everyone, and it also would have figured out what it could do about that situation. Too often, however, congregations refuse to acknowledge changes within their communities until after they have taken place and they're forced to see what they didn't want to face.

Instead of finally saying, "All our people have moved," and then hurriedly trying to buy property to move where members of the congregation have relocated, why can't we do transitioning work? For instance, we could say, "It looks as if in three years the Koreans (or Hispanics or African Americans or Caucasians) will be the majority in this area. Should we start now to reach out to them as they come in? Can we integrate? Do we want to integrate? If we choose not to integrate other cultural and ethnic groups, what can we do to bring about a smooth transition rather than a knee-jerk reaction when we have to face the truth that we should have known three years earlier?"

Mind Transition

An even stronger reason for future thinking is that people need time to work through emotional and ethical issues. Wise leaders provide people with time to transition their minds. None of us just presses mental buttons; we have to adjust our thinking and learn to see from a different perspective.

"What will the future look like?" is a question we in positions of authority need to think through carefully. We need to help those who work under us and with us understand that we can't function effectively with the methods and mind-set of the past.

As I wrote that last statement, it made me wonder how many people in America resisted the automobile. How many refused to buy TV dinners and cake mixes forty years ago? As late as 1999, several of my friends said, "You'll never catch me walking around in public with one of those cell phones." Obviously, people do change their minds, and that alters their behavior. Today I can see some of those once-resistant friends talking on their cell phones as they walk across the church parking lot or through the mall.

My point is that we can't expect most people to make abrupt paradigm changes. We need to remind ourselves that we're not trying to adjust and alter just so we can say, "See, we're different." Our changes need to have a purpose for us to revise our thinking. The major purpose for us as futurefaith people is to become more effective witnesses of Jesus Christ.

This concept reminds me of something J. G. Harlan said: "God gives every bird his food, but he does not

Futurefaith leaders ask two
significant questions.

1. What in my thinking
   needs to change?
2. What keeps me from
   making those
   changes?

throw it into the nest." He meant
that opportunities come to those
who are prepared to receive
them. That's another way to
speak of change readiness.

What I perceive as an opportunity may be part of God's
process in my life. If we're prepared today, God can entrust
more opportunities to us.

We have to ask ourselves, "What did I do today to
ready myself for the future? Is yesterday's preparation
going to carry me through tomorrow? Is there some new
preparation I need to make today to carry me through
tomorrow?"

Another part of change readiness is accepting and
adapting to change. That's difficult for natives, because
they have to start with *unlearning.* In order to embrace
change, they must first unlearn some of their ways of
doing things.

That takes us back to the two questions. First, what
in my thinking needs to change? Second, what keeps
me from making those changes? Natives have been
taught to look backward, and now we're saying, "No,
you can't do that anymore." Thus, some see the futuring church only in terms of having to give up or of having something taken from them. That's the position
some natives choose to take (and it is a choice), because
it is difficult to adjust and to change thinking habits.

The most difficult thing for me in thinking with an
immigrant mind has been and continues to be the
unlearning of old patterns of thinking and outdated
forms of behavior. I've had to learn to relate to people
who have no idea who Hezekiah was or who haven't figured out whether Hebrews is in the Old or New Testament. We used to be able to speak about such things as

the mercy seat, being covered with the blood, being sanctified, or carnal behavior. If I use any of those terms in conversation with immigrants, they look at me as if I'm speaking to them in a foreign language.

Here's an example of how one church—with a large number of natives in the congregation—changed their way of doing evangelism. Trinity Family Worship Church in Rex, Georgia, is located on an arterial highway. Every Tuesday and Thursday for six months, the men of Trinity set up a refreshment stand with free coffee and doughnuts at the edge of their parking lot. They erected a sign that said they were providing free refreshments to people commuting to work. All the commuters had to do was drive into the parking lot, stop, hold out a hand, receive the coffee and doughnuts, and continue their drive to work. They heard no preaching and received no tracts, and no one shouted, "God loves you and so do we."

One regular stop-for-coffee consumer drove a school bus. After she made her final school drop-off, she pulled into the parking lot. Like others, she asked the obvious question: "Why are you doing this?"

"We just wanted to meet you and let you know our church is here," one man said, which was typical of the way any of them answered. "If you want to come to church," he added, "this is where we're located." That was the closest any of the men came to direct evangelism.

When questioned, the men did offer drivers an informational pamphlet about the church, saying, "This will tell you more about us and our programs." They had no ulterior motive. They simply wanted a new way to approach people, to show they were interested in their community, and to respond to the needs of people as they made their way to their jobs. Trinity did receive a number of inquirers and even a few members, but they had chosen to serve coffee and doughnuts even if they never saw a direct benefit. Isn't that the Jesus model of service? We serve others and seek their welfare without expecting anything in return.

Other futuring churches have found excellent ways to reach out to their communities. Counseling programs have been excellent outreach tools, but many churches have discovered that in-house counseling has more liabilities than assets.

- This is especially true if the senior pastor gets involved.
- If the pastor preaches and also does counseling, some of the listeners assume they are the people the pastor is talking about in his illustrations.
- To overcome this criticism, the preacher avoids using what could be meaningful illustrations. Thus, counseling then disempowers the preaching.

Another factor that many congregations have recognized is that the people they help the most in counseling rarely become transformed into the most loyal or faithful. That is, setting up counseling services does not assure an increase in attendance *at that church.* They may, in fact, be recruiting members for another congregation. Research has shown that those who have received counseling may be embarrassed or have other reasons for not joining the church that helped them. They may, however, make their way to another church and become active.

Many futuring churches have studied the need for counseling and agreed that people need such services, so their answer is to outsource counseling. Some contract with counseling services or individual professionals to set up appointments on the church site. Most of the time, those who use the counseling services pay for them but not always. Sometimes a local congregation offers services free or for greatly reduced rates so that more people can take advantage of the therapeutic sessions.

The largest Christian counseling service in the world is called Alpha Care, which is also insurance approved. By hooking up with them or a similar group, churches can provide counseling by outsourcing it to organizations they trust. This arrangement doesn't tie up their staff, somebody else can profit financially, the church and its members are still being serviced, and liabilities are reduced. Doesn't that sound like futuring faith practices at work?

Promoting Change

Leaders promote change through thought, word, and action. In the old days, pastors did everything, including promotion. They announced events from the pulpit and promoted the events they wanted to succeed. Their verbal signature was a signal to church members that said, "This is something you should attend."

We now have many subgroups within the congregation, and each of them needs intentional promoters. No single program can or is intended to appeal to every member. That may sound obvious, but when I was a boy, many churches expected all the faithful members to attend every event; even eighty-year-olds were expected at youth activities. They sat unobtrusively (or so they assumed) in the back during youth services. We learned that if we wanted to be counted among the spiritual, we needed to be present at every activity.

How should promotion within the church work today? Let's say that the pastor and a few deacons believe the congregation should relocate. How should they promote this idea? The most obvious place to start is for the pastor to use pulpit time to advocate moving, and that's how they did it in Daddy's church. But today that's not enough.

Advocacy needs to be done through written media, and just as important, announcements need to be made by promoters within subgroups. Promoters must be strategically selected to deal with the core group, with immigrants, and with natives. That is, they should have leadership among every group and subgroup within the congregation.

Leading Change

When I was thinking about leading change, I scribbled these words:

- Swallow hard and determine to overcome personal reservations of perceived inadequacy and lack of preparation.
- Get out in front and lead.
- If we are going to have change, leaders must be in front of the parade so the crowd knows whom to follow.

"If everything in the world is in transition, why are we—the church—so slow to change?" someone asked.

"We only want to change to a sure thing," I said flippantly. The more I thought about it, however, the more I realized how true my words were.

Change involves risk. For instance, if I'm the CEO of a company and I lead the corporation in change and it works, I'm rewarded with high stock options and a large bonus. If, however, the change sends our stocks downward and profits decrease, I'm out of there and no one remembers my name. And it will be a long time before somebody else gives me a chance to lead a growing organization.

In the church, we tend to be conservative—and a little fearful. We want a sure thing before we make our moves. We want a reasonable guarantee of success. However, in the chaos in which we live, there's never going to be a time when we can make a decision with all the data available. By the time we collect enough data to inform us fully so that we can make a decision, the data has already changed. Because we live in this state of constant flux, change leaders have to move from "change" to "churn." By that, I mean that change is an event, such as moving from point A to point B. *Churn* means we are constantly caught up in chaos. We're continually making adaptations and corrections to the situation.

Timing is important. No longer is there something called "The Plan." Change implementers know the next step, and they probably have a strong concept about the step after that. Some might even be able to foresee step three. After each step, however, they may need to balance everything again. Staff members hired last year may not be the visionaries to take the congregation to the next level of achievement. Deacons elected five years ago may be dragging their feet and holding back the entire congregation.

Leading change is difficult. Change leaders must be sensitive and tough at the same time. For instance, let's say a youth pastor did outstanding work five years ago. Without serious attitude adjustment, that same dynamic person just isn't able to connect with the new group that's coming in. He's now a thirty-five-year-old who's hung up on body piercing, wants all meetings to be Friday evenings from 7:00 to 9:00, and insists on leading the same style of Bible study he did when the church hired him.

Unless he can adapt to the needs of the current teens, he is obsolete. The best thing the congregation can do for him—and for the teens—is to let him go.

I said we need to be tough *and* sensitive. Sensitivity is being aware of the kids who are inching into the youth program. This is a program for *them*. If we're not meeting their needs, we have to exercise toughness by dismissing those who hinder their growth. That nice thirty-five-year-old youth leader was prepared for yesterday and may even have a little preparation for today, but he's not ready for tomorrow. For everyone's sake, including his, we need to let him go unless he keeps up.

This holds true for senior ministers as well. Some pastors need to realize that their threshold is 300 or 500 people. (The issue involves more than the number of people, but I think this illustrates my point.) Sunday morning attendance may reach 550 but will soon fall back to 300, because it will never rise above the senior pastor's ceiling. (For more on this topic, I recommend John Maxwell's *The Twenty-One Irrefutable Laws of Leadership: Follow Them and People Will Follow You*. He discusses the Law of the Lid in reference to a leader's lid, or limit.)

I like to look at this concept in terms of a helium balloon. If I am standing inside a building and release a helium-filled balloon from my hand, the balloon will float upward and stop when it touches the ceiling.

Does the balloon have the capacity to go higher?

Yes.

What holds the balloon down?

The ceiling.

If I want that balloon to rise higher, I have to find a way to raise the ceiling.

Senior pastors are that ceiling, and no congregation can grow beyond the pastor's level of leadership. If the pastor's spiritual growth and leadership skills are stunted by neglect, the church's spiritual and numerical growth will be stunted as well.

Senior ministers tend to hire a larger staff and send the newer personnel to conferences and seminars and insist they read books, listen to tapes, and watch videos. The senior pastors, of course, are too busy "doing ministry."

I would like to ask senior pastors these questions:

> Conductors cannot conduct their orchestra without turning their backs on the crowd. It's not always easy for futuring leaders to turn their backs on the crowd. It is, however, the right thing to do.

1. When was the last time *you* attended a conference for yourself? I'm not referring to the last time you were the keynote speaker, but the time you went to learn and absorb for yourself.
2. What was the last good book you read?
3. When was the last time you read a book?
4. When was the last time you asked tough questions of yourself about change and growth?
5. When was the last time you asked yourself, "What thinking do I need to change?"
6. What is there about me that is hindering the growth of our congregation?

If leaders ask themselves these questions, they can raise the ceiling. For some, the possibilities may be exciting, but for others, the risks seem too great, so the ceiling stays put.

Leading change requires someone to stand at the front to challenge and cheer on others. Leaders are the risk-takers, and they can make life within the congregation challenging and exciting. They lead in change when they themselves begin to grow. If leaders refuse to grow or neglect personal growth, what kind of example are they setting for members of the church?

In summary, change readiness means that leaders must

1. *Prepare* for change.
2. *Promote* change.
3. *Lead* change.

How Work Is Changing

The one-room schoolhouse met the needs of nineteenth-century agrarian culture; institutional-based education and on-site company training met the needs of the office and the manufacturing age of the twentieth century; the working world of the twenty-first century depends on on-line learning.

The following are the major areas of growth in the workplace in this century.

Information on the Job
In 1950 fewer than 100,000 books were in print; fifty years later we estimate that almost that many books are published each year (including self-published and electronic books). This doesn't include Internet sites and other nonbook sources.

There is too much available information for any one person to absorb. A fundamental of success today is having the right kind of information.

Time on the Job
Time is the priceless commodity of the twenty-first century, and wasting time is unacceptable.

Balancing Time

Those who deal with knowledge and information work longer hours than ever. However, not every hour is devoted to work. Those workers try to balance their intense workload with families, leisure-time activities, and community activities.

Work Isn't a Place

Instead of emphasizing work as the place we go, we're now thinking of work as what we do—an activity rather than a place. Because of the Internet and computers, workers are able to do their jobs wherever they're the most productive. Pundits believe that means working at home rather than commuting each day to an office. The office may revolve around the organization's web site, which operates through an *intranet*—a password-protected site on the web.

I'm indebted to the September 2000 issue
of *The New Millennial* for much of this information.

**

The following are six features of how the office work force will operate in this century.

Learning. Workers will spend an hour a day learning, including online learning and conferences.

Next job preparation. One expert says people in information organizations stay an average of five to ten years. Regardless of the length, each job is preparation for the next one workers move into.

Growth of companies. Because of anticipated growth of organizations and their rapidly changing needs, loyalty is dead. Companies need more flexibility and faster turn-around time for new opportunities, and they won't retain workers. They will increasingly contract on a project basis.

Staff definitions. This term becomes difficult to define. The word staff used to refer to full-time, permanent employees. Now it includes part-time employees and contract workers.

Job security. We can forget job security, because increasingly workers will be responsible for their own employment and updating of their skills. Those who have skills that are valuable to the work force will be able to find new jobs.

On-the-job training. The old fear of employers was, "What happens if I train workers and they leave us?" Today the worry is, "What happens if I don't train them and they stay with us?" Because of the changes mentioned above, there is an increasing turnover in the work force, and many will have to leave their jobs because they have not upgraded their skills. Instead of companies training workers, the workers themselves will become increasingly responsible for their continual training.

Source: *The New Millennial,* September 2000, 6

FIVE

Expecting the Unexpected

The second trait of futuring leadership is adaptability. Futuring churches expect the unexpected. They go with the flow around them and continue to redirect their course. They recognize that everything around them is changing and will continue to change.

Nevertheless, the church must adapt to the needs of the real world without forsaking biblical standards. Proponents of alternative lifestyles and other moral issues are challenging the church. Although adaptability doesn't mean moving away from God's mandates, we do need to understand those who don't heed the biblical lifestyle.

For example, at Beulah Heights Bible College, the average student age is 40. The 18-year-olds are a distinct minority. So how do we construct classrooms? Do we keep the old desks—the kind students slid into and out of? Do we provide hard chairs? Do we need chairs with six-inch-foam cushions on the seat?

Immigrants are coming into the church bringing their own values and needs. How do we preach to them? The answer may not be as simple as we think. For example, typically when we preach about the family, we think of the nuclear family—one mother, one father, and children—and we accept that as the norm. But that's no longer the family. Today if a family has two parents, it is most likely a blended family; that is one or both of the parents was previously married and has children from the former marriage. Single-parent families are also on the rise. The 1960 norm is no longer the norm of this millennium.

Another example of change is what is referred to as the graying of America. As a nation, the United States is aging. More people over sixty-five are now alive than at any other time in our history. Each Sunday most pastors preach to three or four generations in the same service.

Such facts mean we must adapt our services and our outreach. The activities we once offered as means of socialization must also change. While we must minister to the graying on one hand, we also have to deal with the fact that 40 percent of the world's population today is under the age of nineteen. Thus, our churches are challenged to reach both ends of the age spectrum. Too many preachers think they can preach one message—that it's still a one-size-fits-all world—and connect with everyone. "This is God's Word," they say defensively. "I proclaim the truth, and God gives the increase."

> "Pastor, if you want to reach me, you better watch your language."
>
> —Ad for a sound system

The purpose of this book is to show the inaccuracy and obsolescence of that mind-set. We who want to lead the futuring church have to learn new styles of leadership, new management techniques, and new technology. Most of us know the language of the natives; now we need to learn the language of the immigrants.

We need to factor in adaptability to changing circumstances. Not only is change coming faster, but it's also coming more frequently and from directions we had not foreseen. In 1970 who would have believed that the biggest agenda item for the church in the first decade of the next millennium would be the issue of sexuality, especially homosexuality?

Who would have imagined that it would have taken Southern Baptists years to decide whether they wanted to keep or oust two congregations that openly accepted homosexuals? In 1995 no one would have believed that they would have considered appointing a committee to study the issue.

"Why would we need to do that?" a native would ask. "We know what's right and we certainly know what's wrong."

Natives Are Certain; Immigrants Aren't Positive

We who believe God's Word and know that any kind of sexual behavior condemned in the Bible is sinful also need to understand that our burden is to find ways— kind and caring ways—to extend the gospel to those most in need as we expect the unexpected.

The Southern Baptists ousted those two churches, and that wasn't the surprise. The surprise was that they did so only after much debate and after they had conducted a study. This illustrates the principle of *expecting the unexpected.*

Years ago we saw the rise in couples living together outside of marriage. We expressed disdain by using derogatory terms for such relationships, including "shacking up." Today the acceptable term is "cohabitation before marriage" and few people blink over the idea. In the past, couples consummated their relationships discreetly, and we assumed they would eventually marry. Today we're seeing more of what I call pre-cohabiting. Couples are sexually active in a monogamous relationship, but the woman has her place and the man has his. Today the woman asks, "Why do I want to give up my home to move in with him? If this relationship doesn't work, I will have lost my home." So now they both keep their homes.

It used to be that as soon as the word *expecting* or *pregnant* entered a couple's vocabulary, they hurried to get married. Today expectant couples often delay getting married or don't marry. Some women are choosing to raise their babies on their own. They say, "He'll be involved because he's the father, but he won't be involved as my husband."

Natives shudder at such a scenario; immigrants know that's part of the real world. Today we expect the unexpected.

I know of a lesbian relationship in which one of the women conceived a child through artificial insemination. The two women now have a baby daughter, and they want to bring her up "in a Christian church atmosphere." What do we tell them if they come to our church?

We need to expect the unexpected.

We used to think of AIDS as a disease that only gays and drug addicts contracted—and only those outside the realm of the church. That's changed; AIDS has now come to church. Many of us began to see it when wives of infected drug users and their babies were diagnosed with the disease.

When those with AIDS do come to church, how do we treat them? Some badly misinformed people still think the disease can be contracted by eating with the same fork or touching the same plate or glass an infected person used. How does the church cope with that? Do we provide separate plates and silverware? How and where do we seat HIV-positive people in our worship services? Do we openly tell people about their situation?

Expect the unexpected.

Once natives learn that another native or an immigrant has AIDS, what happens during times of informal fellowship? Do we hug them? How do mothers feel about that AIDS-infected person who is a gifted teacher of junior kids? Will they allow their children to attend class? Do parents need to know that their child's teacher has AIDS? What kind of disclosure rights or policy does the church have? Must the church tell the parents? If so, where does that leave the infected person? What about his or her right to privacy?

Expect the unexpected.

Shifted Thinking

Every day we are being called on to redirect our course without losing our scriptural moorings and forward momentum. How do we do that?

Not easily.

I like to think of this as a high-wire act in which we constantly make adjustments as we step across the thin wire. Unfortunately for us in the church, there isn't a straight line to follow from point A to point B. We're not even sure where we're going, and we find ourselves zigging and zagging just to keep our balance. As new constructs come up, we're forced to think in new ways. No longer do we think linearly; now we use "looped" thinking, which means that we process numerous complex ideas at a time.

Consider, for instance, the shift we have to make in our thinking concerning the appropriate time for worship. Among futuring churches, 11:00 Sunday morning is no longer the sacred hour of the week. They say, "We can make any hour sacred."

There was a time when churches filled their auditoriums or sanctuaries to capacity at 11:00 then added a second service at 8:30. Some churches even scheduled three or more worship services on Sunday. As I travel around the country and address churches and leaders, I'm seeing an enormous shift from that mentality. I've observed a variety of subgroups, and with the subgroups different needs are being met. Some people may attend the 8:30 service because it is highly liturgical, replete with robes, organ music, and traditional hymns. At the 11:00 service, a band is playing, no one wears robes, and no one opens a hymnal.

Most of the time, young families attend the earliest service. They want to get worship out of the way—not because they're sacrilegious or less devoted, but because they have so many things going on. Yet they do want to start Sunday with their family in church. Leith Anderson points out in his book *Dying for Change* (Bethany, 1990) that 11:00 became the hour of worship when America was a rural, agrarian nation. By that hour, family members could finish their morning chores, hook up their horse to pull the wagon, and arrive at the church down the road. Every Sunday they would spend several hours with their friends and return home just in time to do the evening chores. We haven't been an agrarian or rural culture for at least two generations, yet many churches have fastened on to that nineteenth-century mind-set. Today, however, many service times are changing to reflect the demographics of our communities.

Let's see how this works with the changes in our culture. Martha and Tim finish their jobs on Friday at 5:00.

They have their entire weekend ahead of them. "In order to serve Jesus," Martha asks, "must I tie up my whole weekend? Can't we go to the lake for two days to relax and still have worship in our home church?"

"Yes, Martha, you can do that in futuring churches. In fact, you can become heavily involved in your church and never have to attend on a Sunday—ever."

As she stares wide-eyed, we say, "We have a Friday evening service—it's designed for people like you and Tim."

We've learned that we can do everything on Friday night that we do on Sunday mornings. In fact, we can do it on any day of the week and in a more relaxed atmosphere.

We're also learning that midweek services are more for development and teaching than they used to be. When I was a boy, Wednesday night was just another devotional type of service. If we attended regularly, everyone counted us among the faithful.

Many growing churches no longer have Sunday school. That fact shocks natives. They probably don't know that Sunday school hasn't always been part of Sunday worship. In the late eighteenth century, Robert Raikes developed the idea of Sunday school because of children who worked in factories. It was their day off, and he wanted to teach them to read and write. It's hard to believe now, but the clergy were some of his biggest opponents.

Some immigrant-thinking churches say that Sunday school has outlived its usefulness. Instead, they offer one experience on Sunday and a different one in the middle of the week. These different experiences encompass the full spectrum of needs—from the youngest children to the youth—that is, they are trying to reach every member of each family regardless of the structure of that family unit. Many of these churches also serve dinner before the activities.

Futurefaith leaders have capitalized on the reality that not everyone works from 9:00 to 5:00. Not only do some people work odd shifts, but some, like a friend of mine, work for ten hours a day for four days, have three days off, and then start their week again. Mail carriers work six days and then have the next two days off. In both of these examples, the days off constantly change. Futuring churches plan various events at different times of the day as well as on different days of the week to meet a variety of needs.

When my cowriter, Cec Murphey, was a pastor on the south side of Atlanta, the biggest employer was Delta Airlines, and many of the people in his blue-collar congregation worked shifts. Some of them rotated shifts. He discovered twenty people who were rarely free on Sunday morning, so he started an evening service to reach those specific people. Some of them never attended on Sunday morning, yet they faithfully came every Sunday evening.

In the mornings, futuring churches usually attract stay-at-home moms and mothers with young children. In the afternoons, say from 3:00 to 5:00, congregations can meet the needs of single adults—especially those who are between jobs. They can also stretch out their hands toward those who won't go to work until later and to those who have just left the office or factory for the day.

These examples illustrate that future-thinking congregations no longer devote all their energies to the sacredness of the Sunday morning hour.

Home Churches

On the other hand, a core of people will attend their home church on Sunday morning, regardless of what happens during the week. They're the people who are usually present three out of any four Sundays in a month.

> Futuring church leaders anticipate the unexpected and adapt to changing circumstances.

But many immigrants are not familiar with the home church concept. In expecting the unexpected, futuring leaders may find it helpful to think of them as consumers. They take from each church the things that meet their needs.

Let's say Sylvia has a fifteen-year-old daughter and a seven-year-old son and her husband travels during the week. On Wednesdays Sylvia takes her son to one church and her daughter to another church for a youth group meeting. Sylvia attends a neighborhood Bible study on Wednesday mornings or Thursday afternoons. On most Sunday mornings, Sylvia and her husband worship at the church they joined a decade ago. This family of four has different needs, and they satisfy those needs by attending different churches.

What are the financial implications of this scenario? Where do Sylvia and her husband make their contributions? Do they split their financial pledge, or do they enjoy the services of three churches but give only to one? These are the issues leaders wrestle with—and so do the immigrants themselves.

When we see people like Sylvia attending a church event such as a midweek study but don't see them at Sunday worship, what's going on? The chances are she and her family are going somewhere else on Sunday. They do that because, as I pointed out above, they have different needs. This doesn't mean they are less committed to God.

Maybe they like the choir better at Oak Grove Church or prefer the preaching at Faith Tabernacle. They may even say that the nursery is cleaner at First Baptist than it is at Grace Methodist, and Hope Lutheran has outstanding gym facilities for their teenagers.

Today people are shoppers for their faith. They'll come in, check the facilities, compare the services, and see if that church has something they need. If so, they "buy" by worshiping or serving or simply by staying for that service. Just because they bought something from one church doesn't mean they don't comparison shop.

Futuring leaders know they must be ready to change, and then they adapt to change. There are still eight more qualities they need to embody.

Did You Know?

- Roughly 33 percent of all Americans are over age 50 and one in five is over 65.
- 70,000 Americans are one hundred years old or older.
- The number of centenarians is projected to reach 834,000 by 2050.
- By 2050 many parents and their senior-citizen children will be living in the same retirement community.

Source: U.S. Census Bureau

- Every 7.7 seconds someone turns 50.
- In 2002 more people turned 50 than at any other point in history.

Source: Mary Furlong, ThirdAge Media

- Those 65 and older will double by 2030 to 70 million. During the same period, this group's share of the entire U.S. population will jump from 13 percent to 20.
- Ethnic diversity will increase through 2050.
- The percentage of non-Hispanic whites among older Americans is expected to drop from the current 84 percent to 64.

- In 1950 only 18 percent of older Americans had a high school diploma and 4 percent had at least a four-year degree.

- In 1998 67 percent of older Americans had high school diplomas and 25 percent had at least a bachelor's degree.
- At the beginning of this century, the fastest-growing segment of the working population was workers 55 to 64 while the number of workers in the 16 to 24 age group dropped.

Source: AARP Forum on Aging-related Statistics

- We are facing a blurred ethnicity. By the year 2030, Americans will be so ethnically mixed that few will be able to check one box on the census form under *race*.
- According to a new study reported in the *Atlanta Journal-Constitution*, whites will be a minority in London by 2010.
- According to the Gallup Organization of October 2000, empty-nesters are the fastest-growing group of preretirement households.

SIX

Sensitive Issues

The third trait of futuring leadership is sensitivity—being open and compassionate to everyone. This is a difficult concept for natives to grasp, because many of them have operated for years with a particular set of values (often more cultural than biblical). Too often the response to virtually every question was "The Bible says. . . ." When the Bible doesn't specifically address an issue, many Christians retreat to conservative, cultural attitudes. This isn't to condemn anyone—I grew up among the natives—but it is to say that natives tend to live in a world where the colors are black and white with only the slightest hint of gray. Many immigrants look at the same world, and gray dominates everything.

In the old way of doing things, we drew the lines, set the standards, and decided (tacitly if not actually verbally) the norm for membership in our church. If we're going to stretch into future growth, that's no longer possible. We will be pushed to rethink our biblical foundation, and we may have to smash cultural prejudices.

As we of the futuring church move into the realm of greater sensitivity, we will need to focus on three different kinds of issues—cultural, gender, and generational.

Cultural Issues

The first area that requires our sensitivity is cultural issues. As I implied above, we can no longer make the kind of dogmatic statements that were used in the past. For instance, there was a time in the history of the church when pastors asserted, "If a woman comes to church without her head covered, she is sinning against God." A few months ago I ran into a diatribe written in the 1920s called *Bobbed Hair, Bossy Wives, and Women Preachers.* The title tells us exactly what the author, John R. Rice, had in mind as the normative attitude. In his day and among the native churchgoers, not many people disputed what he had to say.

Cultural sensitivity, however, is more than not being what we were forty or eighty years ago. Cultural sensitivity celebrates differences. It's no longer "us" versus "them." This lack of cultural sensitivity (even appreciation) is one of the great impediments to the growth of any congregation, no matter what the size, the language, or the country. As long as we think of "those people" and "us," we're impeding the advance of God's kingdom. In fact, this is probably the greatest impediment to assimilation that leads to healthy growth.

Cec Murphey says that in his pastoral days, some of the older natives referred to "our kind of people" and the people who "don't belong here." He said it was a constant tension to affirm the natives and let them know they were loved and valued while he wrapped his arms around immigrants. No matter how hard he tried, for some of the people—both natives and immigrants—there was always a split. He discovered that some of the natives assumed that it was their right to receive more time and attention because they had been in the church longer. If they were second- or third-generation members, they felt entitled to even more time and privileges. That meant they kept the immigrants at an emotional distance until the newcomers proved themselves and became "one of us." That situation probably wouldn't happen today in a futuring church where people deliberately choose to celebrate their diversity rather than try to make everyone look, dress, and speak exactly alike.

> Cultural sensitivity celebrates diversity. The greatest impediment to growth is to maintain an us-and-them attitude.

Cultural sensitivity isn't merely about Koreans, Latinos, African Americans, and Caucasians all worshiping in the same room, although that may be the most conspicuous example. I'm referring to different socioeconomic cultures, such as blue-collar workers and professionals. For example, my cowriter was once invited to become the pastor in a mill town in Alabama. There was another church there of the same denomination, and they told Cec, "Management goes to our church. Workers and hourly wage people attend the other." (He chose not to accept the invitation.)

Today we have northerners who have moved south and easterners who have gone west. It's more than a physical move, because we take our cultures with us. I can show this cultural difference better by pointing to the matter of funerals.

- When I was a pastor in Michigan, people visited the funeral home (or mortuary then), and the locals called it a viewing. In the South, they call it visitation.

- In the North, it was never a big thing to conduct a funeral on Sunday. In the Deep South, there must be some extenuating circumstances for that to happen.
- In the North, people are more likely to attend the viewing, where they pay their respects to the family. Consequently, attendance at funerals is not as large as in the South. In the South, it's the reverse.
- In the North, a hearse drives down the road with an entourage behind it, and people scarcely pay any attention. In many parts of the South, drivers pull off the road until the entire procession has passed.

Mix cultural differences with various educational backgrounds, blend in the social culture, and then add the ethnic background. Is it any wonder we've awakened to diversity in our churches?

Here are two other ways to see this.

Humor. Pastors and other church leaders need to understand that what once seemed funny may not be a harmless joke today. We don't tell stories about the Polish, the Irish, or Mexicans. A few insensitive people still take on an accent, speak condescendingly, and assume they're funny. Some church leaders still tell jokes that put down marriage—the very sacred rite they yearn to protect.

Homecoming events. In the past, many churches celebrated the birth of their congregations by bringing food and having dinner on the grounds. But if we're culturally and racially diverse, how do we make Filipinos, Latinos, and Vietnamese feel part of that celebration? How do we build cultural bridges for everyone to cross over?

One thing we do at Beulah Heights to build a cultural bridge is to have a yearly celebration we call Taste of the

Nations. We spend the morning in chapel, and international students conduct the service and prepare food to share afterward. In 2001 twenty-five countries were represented in our college. They brought their music, sang, played instruments, and many of them wore their national dress. Some of them danced to their music. Then we went outside to a large open area where we had tables set up with food from every country represented.

The Student Government Association pays international students to prepare the food so that we don't impoverish any students. That's a major point of sensitivity. Instead of saying, "Bring the food," our student government has been culturally sensitive enough to say, "We have students here, and some of them barely scrape by. We want Odera from Kenya to cook a large batch of ugali, so we'll give him the money to buy the ingredients." In short, we support the international students financially so they can work with us to build the bridge.

Another thing we do at Beulah Heights to build a cultural bridge is to hold a yearly all-staff meeting at which we expect everyone to be present. I talk about the issues we face in a multicultural, international school. At the first meeting, I said, "Did you know that talking louder does not make the students understand English any better?" Although a few laughed, I had observed that a few staff members raised their voices to a higher decibel to be understood. "You know what?" I said. "That device doesn't change anything. They are not hearing impaired."

Gender Issues

The second area that requires sensitivity is gender issues. I believe that the gifts and callings of God are gender inclusive and not gender exclusive. I realize that there are still many who oppose my point of view. I can accept them and their position, and I hope they can accept me and mine. My position is that God calls a person to ministry, and it has nothing to do with that person's gender. In some roles, however, one gender or the other may be more efficient.

There are always exceptions, but *generally speaking*— and much of this may come from our cultural background and teaching—men and women think differently. If that's true, they also tend to lead differently.

- Men tend to lead by position, and women tend to lead by relationships.
- Men tend to exercise knowledge; women tend to rely on intuition.
- Men tend to focus on getting the job done; women tend to focus on involving everyone—being more inclusive and more relational.
- Men may want to fix the problem, while women may be very good at hearing, sympathizing, and empathizing.
- Men may want issues to be clear-cut, but many women can see deeper implications.

What role should gender play in the way positions are filled at church? Suppose we need another helper in the nursery. Do we say, "We need a woman to assist in the nursery?" Men can be good fathers and caregivers, can't they? So why must we make the invitation gender specific?

Isn't it a bit insulting and archaic to say "male nurse," "female lawyer," or "male flight attendant"?

A few years ago, two of my receptionists left and I had to replace them. Until then we had hired only female receptionists, a custom we had inherited from the past. This time I intentionally screened candidates and hired two male receptionists to replace two females. That was a paradigm shift. When people called Beulah Heights for the first time, they expected to hear a woman answer. We laughed when our new receptionists initially experienced a number of awkward pauses and even a few hang-ups.

In 2001 I had to hire a financial aid director. I wanted to employ an African-American woman—again, that was something we had never done at Beulah Heights. I wanted a black director because our school is predominantly African American. I wanted to avoid having needy black students come to the financial aid office and sit down in front of a white person, especially if that person had to say no. I wanted no cries of racial prejudice. And I wanted a woman because 55 percent of our student body is female. Another reason I wanted to hire a woman was because I needed someone who was able to be firm when she had to be, but could also hold the hand of those who needed it.

In summary, on the matter of gender sensitivity, futuring church leaders open up and explore possibilities. They are not locked into selecting a specific gender for specific tasks. They are more interested in function and ability than gender.

Generational Issues

The third area in which futuring leaders must be sensitive is the generational gap. Paul Star wrote in an article called "Clueless" for the *American Prospect,* May 8, 2000:

We are in a new generational territory here. One day last year at a class at Princeton on American society where we were discussing the 1960s I asked my students what the phrase "generational gap" brought to mind. If you think it has anything to do with sex, drugs, and rock and roll, you're probably much older than 28. The first answer from the class was technology. Then a young woman said that her parent's generation wasn't as entrepreneurial as hers.

The term *generational gap* has been redefined. We have more generations in our church now than we did ten years ago. Thus, we have to ask, "How will the structure, ministry, and leadership be able to meet the needs of all those generations?"

Perhaps a personal illustration will help. When I was a pastor in 1985, a woman would come to our church, seek out the nursery, and leave her baby there. That was the norm. Now in a more highly sensitized culture in which people are aware of all the abuse that has taken place, parents don't want to walk into church and leave their babies in the hands of people they don't know. Furthermore, church leaders today don't allow anyone to work in the nursery without a background check.

Other new trends in nursery care show a sensitivity to parents. For instance, when parents drop off their children, they take with them a low-frequency beeper. If the nursery workers need the parent, they use the beeper—which doesn't actually beep but vibrates.

Nursery workers today perform on a highly professional level. Many even wear white smocks over their clothes to project an image of professionalism. They don't just hand children back to their parents, but during the last half of the worship service, they spend much of their time cleaning up, changing diapers, and doing everything necessary to send children home clean, dry, and fed. This is an excellent example of sensitivity to generations, for the level of care today's parents expect is higher than in any previous generation.

Futuring leaders continue to grow. They become aware of their need to change, they adapt by expecting the unexpected, and they become sensitive to the issues they face—and some of those are situations they've never wrestled with before. They then have to figure out how to express their new understandings.

Futuring leaders continue to grow by staying aware of emerging sensitive issues. This sensitivity enables them to change, to adapt to the future by expecting the unexpected at a deeper level, especially as they venture into territories yet to be explored.

SEVEN

Communication Today

The fourth trait of futuring leaders is effective communication. For our communication to be effective today, it must cut across generations, cultures, and even across the globe. The biggest dilemma in communication is that each generation communicates and reacts to communication differently—and too often communicators don't realize that their words have gone past their intended receivers.

Generational Communication

Perhaps the easiest way to explain the problems of generational communication is to use the terms sociologists use to distinguish the generations—*seniors, builders, boomers, busters,* and *mosaics.* In the table below, I show the general attitudes and characteristics of each group.

Leadership and Five Generations

Leadership Issue	Seniors	Builders	Boomers	Busters (Gen-X)	Mosaics (Nexters)
Era Born	Before 1928	1929–45	1946–64	1965–83	1984–2002
Life Paradigm	Manifest Destiny	Be grateful you have a job	You owe me	Relate to me	Life is a cafeteria
Attitude toward Authority	Respect	Endure	Replace	Ignore	Choose
Role of Relationships	Long term	Significant, useful	Limited, caring	Central	Global
Value System	Traditional	Conservative	Self-based	Changing	Shop around
Role of Career	Loyal, responsible	Means for living	Central focus	Irritant	Always changing
Schedules	What's up?	Mellow	Frantic	Aimless	Volatile
Technology	What's that?	Hope to outlive it	Master it	Enjoy it	Employ it
View of Future	Uncertain	Seek to stabilize	Create it!	Hopeless	??

1. *Seniors* refers to anyone born before 1928. Some place them before 1930. The exact year of birth of people in these categories isn't the issue as much as their socialization and general attitudes. The socialization of seniors focused on the Great Depression, Franklin Roosevelt's administration, and World War II. They grew up during a time of relative unity in the nation and with a common core of values. With few exceptions, they are the retired generation. Because of the Great Depression experience, many worry about whether they will have

enough money to pay their medical bills and sometimes fear that Social Security and Medicare will fail them.

2. *Builders* refers to the next generation, who came just before the baby boomers. Many of them remember World War II, and all of them can talk about the Korean Conflict. They liked Ike for president and remember the day John Kennedy died. That is, they were born anywhere between the late 1920s and 1945. Builders say, "Be grateful you have a job." They're less concerned about what they do or how fulfilling it may be and more concerned with having work and a paycheck. "Just endure if you don't like what you're doing."

3. *Boomers (or baby boomers)* are those born between 1946 and 1964. Their attitude is likely to be, "You owe me a job. Give me a good one." These are the offspring of the two older generations. They grew up with Elvis and the Beatles. Most of them had strong feelings about the Vietnam War, which added words such as Agent Orange and Post-Traumatic Stress Disorder (PTSD) to the nation's vocabulary. Their parents had worked to give them a better life, and they learned to expect higher standards of living. Instead of buying small houses and older cars, they say, "I deserve to have the best now."

Did you know? Most people under the age of 40 don't know what "cc" on a memo stands for.

4. *Busters (or Gen-X)*, those born approximately between 1965 and 1983, say, "Ignore them." This generation of more than 40 million is the offspring of the baby boomers, a population of 77 million Americans. They tend to be serious about life and therefore give consideration to critical decisions. They are also stressed out. School, family, peer pressure, sexuality, techno-stress, finances, high crime, and even political correctness contribute to their stressful lives. Yet they aren't driven toward success as much as their

Why are busters or Gen-X a smaller population than their parents, the boomers?

Here are six contributing factors:

1. The United States became the center for the world's highest divorce rate.
2. Birth-control methods became increasingly common and accessible, especially with the availability of the pill.
3. Abortion reached a rate of 1.5 million each year.
4. A college education became accessible to more people, especially women who slowly moved into influential positions in the workforce.
5. Social change, including women's liberation (or the feminists' movement), encouraged more women to consider careers instead of "just" being homemakers.
6. The economy led many women to work because they had to or because they became the sole breadwinners.

predecessors. They are self-reliant, believing they can make sense out of their religious faith. This doesn't mean they focus on Christianity; rather, they tend toward a broader view of "spirituality." And at the same time, they're skeptical—which may be a defense against disappointment.

5. *Mosaics (or Nexters)*, born between 1984 and 2002, are well acquainted with technology and are looking for ways to use it. Their attitude toward work moves from mastering tasks, to making money with their skills, to using that money. Until the destruction of the World Trade Center in 2001, Desert Storm was the only American military involvement they personally experienced. They're labeled mosaics because of their eclectic lifestyle, their nonlinear thinking, the fluidity of their

personal relationships, and what someone has called their "hybrid spiritual perspective." They baffle their elders by their comfort with contradictions related to everything from spirituality to morality to families and politics. They will enthusiastically pursue spiritual goals, but they are less likely to feel constrained by traditional theological parameters. They are also the most information-overloaded generation.

A large number of this generation saw their parents lose their jobs due to downsizing. Thus, they distrust institutions. They are also the first generation to be socially active since the 1960s. They bring their social-conscious values to the workplace.

Generational Cultures

This five-generation span also reflects the speed of communication. E-mail is both a terrific blessing and a horrible curse. It's terrific because it has accelerated communication; but it's terrible because it has accelerated *mis*communication and *mis*information. What used to take a week to travel around the globe now can be spread within hours—long before the accuracy of the content has been verified.

I've discovered several web sites devoted just to listing hoaxes and bogus virus threats, often called urban legends. Too many people spread the message without looking at such web sites, and some probably don't even know they exist. Too often they operate out of panic and perpetuate rumors and encourage fear.

Here's an example of what I mean. About 1980, only a few years before the common use of the computer, thousands of Christians became upset because someone circulated a letter saying that the Federal Communications Commission (FCC), under the influence of

Madalyn Murray O'Hair, was going to stop all religious programming. These outraged Christians urged people to sign petitions to send to the FCC. The FCC made a public announcement that it was a hoax and that the tons of mail they had received was a wasted effort.

Nevertheless, old hoaxes refuse to die. In the late 1990s, people began receiving e-mails with essentially the same message that had once circulated in paper form. They warned that the FCC was going to stop all religious programming and that this action had been inspired by the efforts of Madalyn Murray O'Hair. (O'Hair was already dead before the e-mail rumors flew, and most alert people, even if they didn't know she was dead, knew she had been missing.) Can you imagine what the e-mails urged? They pleaded with readers to flood the FCC with protest letters.

A year later, a similar e-mail message circulated saying that the TV series *Touched by an Angel* would be taken off CBS because they used the word *God* in the program. Again the writer asked for letters of protest. One form of the e-mail even urged readers to add their names and addresses and forward the petition to "everyone on your mailing list." (I wonder what smart advertisers made use of that list!) A few people questioned the truthfulness of those e-mails but apparently not many. In the meantime, panicked Christians did just what they were told to do—they sent copies of the letter to everyone on their list. Because the hoax came out in print (on the screen, e-mail counts as print), many gullible people never questioned the truthfulness of what they read.

Another less obvious but dangerous problem with e-mail is that it can be responsible for the increase of conflict. When we did more snail-mailing, people tended to take time to think through what they wanted to say before they put paper in their typewriter or got out their stationery. Today it's easy to read an e-mail, react, and dash off an answer. In many cases, the immediate response creates conflict because of hurried reading or frenzied responding.

If someone comes to my office, sits down across from my desk, and says, "I disagree with you, Sam," I can begin to deal with that difference. I hear the voice and observe the body language. This is true for all of us, because we interact and involve ourselves with more than just the words. E-mail, however, doesn't give us that luxury. We may automatically dash off a response—and then have to send a series of e-mails to correct our miscommunication.

E-mailing affects the church in many ways. Who is sending out the information? Does it come from an authorized "server"? Can everyone send whatever e-mails they want to the entire membership? Is it all right for the entire congregation to receive messages from a member who has access to their e-mail addresses and uses that to spread information? What happens if the message sent, even from an authorized person, is misunderstood or misinterpreted? I assure you, this does happen—all the time.

Intra-office communication is another problem area. Suppose a deacon comes into the church kitchen and sees two frying pans left in the wrong place. Maybe there's a Coke can left in a window. The angry deacon fires a heated note by intra-office memo.

· The receiver gets the memo, reads it hurriedly, and bumps back a response. "They are only teens. Be thankful the place is as clean as it is."

Instead of such trivial issues (and such things do happen) being worked out between leadership and the person(s) responsible, they end up spreading among people who don't need to be involved.

During my years of being a pastor, irate church members had two major means of complaint *without* a face-to-face confrontation. Some chose to use the telephone, and most of the time they were willing to listen for an explanation. Others who wouldn't express strong negative feelings directly chose to write angry letters that came to me via snail mail. Occasionally they pushed envelopes under my door when they came to a church meeting. Most of the time, however, it took at least twenty-four hours before I received and read their angry messages. Sometimes their letters hurt, shocked, or disappointed me. I was surprised that these people would react in such petty ways—and for such trivial reasons.

The one advantage I had was time. The delay gave me the opportunity to reflect on what I read, and I was able to think about their needs and concerns. I also had choices on how to respond. I could send back a letter, and that might take as long as three more days, or I could wait a few hours and call the person on the phone. The passing of time can often have a significant healing effect. When I did get back to an irate member, hours or days had passed and the person's anger had usually cooled.

Today the complaints come faster, almost instantaneously. For those unwilling or unable to express anger directly, e-mail is the method. They dash off a few sentences and click the send button.

For example, at 1:00 on Sunday afternoon, an angry usher e-mails me to tell me that I did something wrong or said words that offended somebody during the worship service. I casually check my e-mail at about 2:45, and there's the message staring at me—less than two hours after the event. I'm ready to fire off an equally angry response. Unless I pause, reflect, and hold my temper, I'm apt to send a harsh or heated reply, and that, in turn, may provoke an even stronger response.

The speed with which these complaints and rapid-fire responses are sent increases the possibility of anger intensifying.

My point is that we have changed from a culture that moves slowly to one that is nearly instant. This lays a heavy burden on us to communicate thoughtfully and clearly. I urge people to pause and reflect before typing out a hurried message. In fact, the more urgent I feel about a message, the more slowly I need to respond. Before I press the send button, it helps to ask, "How will he (or she) respond to this e-mail?"

Too many people forget the common rules of kindness and consideration when they pound out their e-mails. Perhaps before we send the next e-mail or intra-office communication either in anger or in response to anger, it may help to think of these words spoken by Jesus:

> Love your enemies! Pray for those who persecute you! In that way, you will be acting as true children of your Father in heaven. . . . If you love only those who love you, what good is that? Even corrupt tax collectors do that much. If you are kind only to your friends, how are you different from anyone else? Even pagans do that.
>
> Matthew 5:44–47 NLT

Communication across Cultures

Anyone who has traveled in other countries knows that we have gestures and speech patterns that are not universally understood. For instance, Americans gesture "OK" by forming a circle with the thumb and index finger, but in South America, that is an obscene gesture.

We think nothing of accepting gifts or doing actions with our right hand or our left, because in the United

States, there is no difference. In some cultures, however, it is an insult to offer or receive with the left hand.

> Leaders need to recognize differences in communication among different age groups. Communication needs to cross generations, cultures, and geography.

For example, one church member of an Anglican-type congregation in Hyderabad, India, angrily criticized Cec Murphey for his actions. After Cec preached the morning service, he assisted the rector in serving the Eucharist. People came forward and knelt in front of the altar, and the priest offered each a sip from the wine goblet. Cec followed behind with the plate of bread. He is ambidextrous and wasn't aware that he was offering the plate with his left hand. That is, he wasn't aware until one member pulled him aside after the service and berated him for "insulting the people of India."

Words also have different meanings. For instance, the term for a female dog seems to be offensive only in America, but some of our harmless words cause offense in other cultures. In England some consider *bloody* as a vulgar expression.

EIGHT

Technophilia
vs. Technophobia

The fifth characteristic of futuring leaders is that they are not only aware of emerging technology, but they also quickly adopt its use. In this chapter I discuss three types of technology:

1. Information technology.
2. Industrial technology.
3. Business technology.

(Churches, of course, primarily use informational technology.)

Technophilia is the term I use to refer to friendliness and openness to technology. Long gone are the days when anyone argued over whether to adapt to the electronic world. The war is over, and technology won. Our question is: What do we do with technology in the church?

Churches in general have been slow to embrace technology, but futuring leaders urge us to recognize that technology makes information available to us that we didn't have before. As they say in the business world, "Information is power." Technology provides us with tools we can use to reach people for and teach people about Jesus Christ.

Informational Technology

In the past, we church leaders received most of our information from denominational headquarters, or if we belonged to an independent church, we had a loose-knit network from which we received information formally and informally. In any case, our information sources were fairly limited. Because "this ain't our daddy's church anymore," futurefaith leaders urge us to expand our information sources.

I personally do a number of things to get more information. I subscribe to an audiotape service and listen to those tapes when I'm driving, and I'm signed up with three different free e-mail leadership services. Other online resources are also available, such as Leadership Network, which provides a variety of information about the church. George Barna has a free newsletter that summarizes his findings of social impact on the church. Another free newsletter called *Netfax* is about emerging trends.

I also have three paid subscriptions to e-mail newsletters. My favorite is *LN BookNotes* by George Bullard. He writes in-depth book reviews and offers insights from the books themselves, enabling me to know what is available, what a book is about, and whether I should buy a copy.

Industrial Technology

Perceptive pastors are now asking themselves three questions:

1. What technology do we have right now?
2. What technology do we have right now that needs improving?
3. What new technology can enhance what we're already doing?

Consider, for example, the microphone, which is standard in just about any church today. How can we improve that? We can use hand-held wireless mikes. How can we improve that? We can use lavaliere mikes or headsets. These are the kinds of questions a leader has to continually ask.

Moreover, we should also reexamine the sound system, the taping system, and the video system. We use industrial technology in an industrial world. This is ministry, of course, and we need little to remind us of that. Nevertheless, it's also industry—and even if we don't like it, we function that way. Thus, we must harness any technology that will enhance our ministry.

Business Technology

How do we conduct the business of the church? How do we transmit information? One technological help is the phone tree, a machine no larger than a tape recorder. All we do is go through a zip sorter and enter everyone's phone number into it. For example, like a mass e-mail, the phone tree calls every high school senior and says, "Don't forget the seniors' banquet is Friday night at 7:00."

> **Technology nudges futuring leaders to ask:**
>
> 1. What technology do we have right now?
> 2. What technology do we have that needs improving?
> 3. What new technology can enhance what we're already doing?

The system we use at **BHBC** will record on an answering machine. If our machine gets a busy signal, it will call back three times. The phone tree also keeps a log (which we can print out) of which numbers remained busy or simply didn't answer.

In the South where I live, about once a year we have an ice storm or snowstorm. Because we don't have good equipment to clean the streets, most of the city shuts down for a day. Sometimes churches have had to call off their morning services due to a storm. Large churches could record a message saying that the church service is canceled and use the phone tree to call every member's home.

Furthermore, we need to find out what kinds of business software will make our churches run more efficiently. What accounting software is available for churches? How can members receive their contribution receipts before January 31 and know they're accurate? How can pastors keep track of visitors and be able to compile and analyze other demographics as well? Business technology almost makes redundant some questions on the visitors' card. If visitors write down only their names and phone numbers, that's all we need. By using the Internet, we can find out where they live and even download directions to their homes. We can also use technology to do our church bulletin by e-mail.

If we don't keep up with technology, the immigrants come, look around, and say, "I don't get it." Or they act as if they've stepped into an outdated church environment, and they treat us accordingly.

"The church is irrelevant" is something we've heard often in recent years. To make a positive impact on that

Is Your Church Accessible?

The Barna Research Group phoned 3,764 randomly selected Protestant congregations in June and July of 2000. They wanted to learn the availability of the church. Results? They said they were unable to establish contact with anyone at 40 percent of the churches despite repeated attempts. Nearly half of them where no person could be contacted didn't even have answering machines. In other cases where Barna's people left messages, they went unanswered.

"In a world where people are extremely busy and are suspicious of the practical value of churches, they are not likely to make three or four calls to a church before they get to speak to a human being," George Barna said. "If churches want to help people, they have to be accessible."

kind of thinking, we have to be better prepared to minister in a culture where at least 10 percent of the population will abandon the physical church building for an exclusively digital faith experience. George Barna has warned, "Churches that don't make technology part of their arsenal of tools will die after the last of their antitechno members dies 20 years from now. It will be a needlessly painful death for those ministries."

As futuring leaders we know the first five things we need:

1. We prepare for change.
2. We realize we can't plan the future because the unexpected continues to happen.
3. We remain abreast of sensitive issues.
4. We become modern communicators.
5. We're not afraid of technology. In fact, we learn and use it to spread the good news of Jesus Christ.

NINE

Healthy Lifestyles

The sixth trait of futuring leadership is what I call healthy lifestyles. In this chapter, I emphasize balance, behavior, and biotechnology.

Balance

I use the term *balance* to refer to such things as rest, proper diet, exercise, leisure, and companionship. We may never be perfectly balanced, but I believe working toward equilibrium brings us as close to being balanced people as we'll come in this age.

Because of our frazzled lifestyles today, everyone seeks balance. We're all being pulled in several directions at once. Forces outside of us jerk us around. We have more demands pulling at us today than we had yesterday, and we tend to respond to the "tyranny of the urgent," that is to the immediate cry even if it's not as important as something else. How can we alleviate stress? How can we change our behavior to handle daily crises?

I travel a lot. At the time I started writing this book, I had just returned from ten days of travel that included six outbound flights. That means I had been on planes twelve times in ten days. What is it about my behavior that allows me to have a healthy lifestyle? How do I avoid the hassle and stress so many feel when they rush to the airport, stand in line, go through security checks, and finally board the plane? I get to the airport early, pick out my place to sit, open my briefcase, and get a lot of work done. Instead of moaning about the interminable wait, I focus on tasks I want to accomplish and thus I avoid feeling that my work won't get done or that I'm wasting time. I'm relaxed when I board the plane.

> People seek balance as they struggle with issues such as rest, meals, exercise, leisure, and companionship. Leaders need to ask themselves how to meet those needs.

By contrast, I have several friends who brag about how they race to the airport, hurry down the hallways, and rush onto the plane during the final boarding call. They don't tell me how frazzled they are the rest of the day or about the stress that builds up in them.

I've used these behavioral patterns for illustration. We can always change our behavioral patterns. Part of balance is to remind ourselves that our bodies belong to God and that we are holy temples. We're responsible for our lifestyles, and we can do a great deal toward controlling our stress levels. We also need to remind ourselves that when we live continually stressful lives, our health and our attitude are affected as well as our effectiveness for God.

Behavior

How do I modify my behavior to meet the changing needs in my life? Above I gave the example of reaching the airport early as one stress in life that I can control. But what about my behavior when I'm with my family or at work? I behave differently with different people. At noon, for instance, I may interact with a close friend. I can laugh, plan, disagree, cry, or share and can become vulnerable in many ways. When I respond to a staff member, however, my behavior will be different. Nothing changes in respect or courtesy, but the dynamics do. When I'm talking to staff people, I am the boss. An acceptable code of behavior is in place in most situations. If I have to speak to my board, the dynamics change once again.

Biotechnology

Pastoral care is changing. One way to show this is to think about a brain-damaged child. In the past, parents prayed and asked for healing prayer in church, went to faith healers, or simply allowed nature to take its course. Many of them shielded their offspring from stares and ridicule by excluding them from many forms of socialization.

Today those parents take their children to a doctor who refers them to specialists. Current technology now provides life-support systems and a wide range of medication. How do we relate to such children in our churches?

One congregation I know of has a Sunday school class for those we once labeled mentally retarded. The dozen regular members feel proud to be part of a class—to belong to a group where they feel safe and supported.

Think about the nine-year-old child who can't breathe without a respirator. Her parents have learned to hook up the oxygen tank when they take her out in a wheelchair. A generation ago, she probably wouldn't even have lived this long. Where does pastoral counseling come in, and how can the church help the child? What can the church do for the parents?

People today are living longer. Technology has provided a way for many people to live beyond their normal life spans. Fifty years ago, great numbers of people died in infancy. This means that we have more older people alive than at any other time in our nation's history. That alone changes the face of pastoral care.

How do we care for older parishioners? I don't mean just sending them a tape of the service along with a copy of the Sunday bulletin. Today many are in transitional homes, skilled-nursing facilities, or assisted-living environments, so how do we provide substantial pastoral care?

We also need to minister to people who care for their ailing parents. Caring for a parent who has dementia or Alzheimer's disease can be very trying. We must also become sensitive to families that are financially stressed because of long-term illness or nursing care.

As futuring leaders increase their ability to grow and lead, they stress healthy lifestyles and teach others how to find balance. And as they help others cope in their struggle for balance, they become increasingly aware of their own need to make learning a lifelong practice.

TEN

Lifelong Learning

The seventh trait of futuring leaders is that they are life-long learners.

Three significant factors about life today show a drastic shift in attitude over the generations.

1. Knowledge is power.
2. Information is currency.
3. Innovation is success.

Twenty years ago we encouraged (even pushed) our young people to get a college degree. The idea was that graduation completed formal education, and for many that is exactly the way it was. "I haven't read a book since I graduated from college," we used to hear people say with pride.

Today the degree seems less important, but learning doesn't stop. Our technological world is built on the idea of lifelong education. We can't stop learning. For instance, if my daughter earns a Master of Science in computer information systems from the most prestigious institution on this planet, within six months her education will be obsolete unless she is committed to lifelong learning.

A decade ago, some large companies could afford the luxury of paying for their employees to go to workshops, seminars, and classes to pick up continuing education units. That's no longer a luxury. If workers want to continue to do well in their jobs, they have to keep growing and learning even if they have to pay for the classes themselves.

Church leaders also need to be committed to more reading and to lifelong learning with a broader base. In the past, they read a few theological magazines—and nearly always the kind that agreed with their theological position. That's too narrow for today. Now they need to know what's going on in the world and relate to it. After the destruction of the World Trade Center in 2001, bookstores and libraries were overwhelmed with requests for information about Islam. Not many pastors were knowledgeable enough to teach such a course. Instead, people went to mosques, bought books by secular writers, and enrolled in seminars and workshops to learn more about Islam. Many churches missed a great opportunity.

Futuring leaders not only have to be aware of current Christian literature, but they also need to read or at least be conversant with non-Christian literature. There was a time when godly Christians didn't read fiction, and if they did, it was only wholesome evangelistic stories. That has changed. The proliferation and range of novels have shattered many naïve people when they have realized the broadness of the audience. Today smart leaders know what's coming off the presses in fiction and nonfiction.

Because they keep up, they can answer questions about reincarnation or communicating with the dead.

Every major secular publishing house now has what they call a spiritual or Christian imprint—and well-known evangelical writers write many of the books they publish. Why this interest? It's because we're in an age of spirituality, and books on spiritual topics sell. The category *spirituality*, however, includes everything from yoga to Taoism to Wiccan literature to Buddhism to every aspect of Christianity.

Increasingly, niche-oriented journals are coming out. They have a faster turnaround rate and can pump out information far more quickly than book publishers.

> Someone said, "It takes a long time to prove to people that you're smart. It only takes a split second to prove that you're ignorant."

If we're lifelong learners, not only will we be able to catch our mistakes and missteps, but we'll also be able to know what to do about correcting them. In a family, for example, lifelong learners recognize the difference between punishing and disciplining their children. Punishment is punitive; discipline is corrective and prepares them to do better next time. Punishment focuses only on behavior now, and discipline instructs for the future.

In the old days, a dad typically said to his son, "You did wrong, and you knew it. Now, as your loving parent, I must punish you." Today a parent may say, "Maybe you shouldn't have done that. I want to tell you a better way to handle that situation the next time it happens." That father is focusing on lifelong learning for the child. Lifelong learners realize that the important question isn't "What difficulties did we go through?" It is, "What did we learn as we went through hardships?"

I'm thankful that God provides the best lifelong learning. In our schools and colleges, we are taught a lesson

---

What Are We Saying?

If you're over forty, you've probably heard the statements below. Maybe you have used them with your own children because you heard them from your parents. What are the messages we're communicating with these words?

"Do as I say, not as I do."
"You want to be *what?*"
"Your room is a pigsty."
"Can't you do anything right?"
"I'm busy right now. Can you come back later?"
"Where did you find *him* (or *her*)?"

---

and then are tested on our own. God's way of doing things is to give us the test, stay at our side while we go through the ordeal, and gently embrace us, asking, "What have you learned from this experience?" Thus, with God our learning grows out of our testing.

Let's see how this concept works in the church by looking at styles of leadership. In the past, we accepted (and sometimes even desired) autocratic leaders. Today that style just isn't working. Some leaders keep trying, but it doesn't work for them to stand up and make pronouncements for everyone. Because they keep trying and keep failing, they are punished by lack of results. Increasingly, their critics speak out against them. The leaders themselves still haven't learned anything and one of their defenses is to resort to blame, which supposedly takes the focus off themselves and shines the spotlight on others. They say things like,

"People aren't as spiritual today as they used to be."
"Church members today don't want to hear what God says."

"The Bible warns us of itching ears, and there are a lot of them in the church today."

"They're not just rejecting me, they're rejecting the Word of God."

As long as leaders blame others for their failures, see themselves as the final voice on all issues, and insist on being *the* leader, nothing much is going to change. However, if they listen to others, accept guidance and rebuke, and seriously study the needs of others, they will start to acknowledge that their methods just aren't effective. If they can be that open with themselves, they'll also acknowledge that failure is not because of people's hardness of heart, but because people today don't respond to a demanding style of leadership.

"How can I reframe, refocus, reinvent, or reenergize my message?" is the question futuring church leaders are asking. They no longer assume that people are indifferent, uncaring, and stiff-necked. Instead, they figure out what people don't respond to and recognize that it was often their style of leadership. As they continue to learn, they ask, "What approach can I take that people will understand and accept as supportive? How can I do ministry differently?" They may even say to themselves, "Maybe I need a champion—someone who can support my cause."

Changing leadership styles is a real test for many leaders because they have always been at the center of all activity and they're uncomfortable if they're not in charge. One thing they'll learn is that it doesn't matter who gets credit for initiating ideas or even carrying them out. The effective results are what count.

Not all leadership styles can accommodate that openness, but it's something I've learned to do. I think it's because, when I pastored, I learned that instead of thinking of leadership as power, I functioned better if I considered leadership as influence. The best leaders are those who motivate, suggest, and encourage but who don't demand, tell, or insist.

Here's what I mean by influence. I had an idea of something that I wanted to happen at Beulah Heights Bible College, but it was controversial. Because my idea was costly, it was apt to encounter resistance.

> Working in teams requires a paradigm shift—a new way of thinking. We have to be able to admit that what we were positive we knew isn't necessarily so.

I called a member of the board and asked if we could have lunch. I chose him because he is highly respected by me and by the other members. I wanted his input. If he liked what I proposed, I could count on his influencing the others.

After I explained what I had in mind, I asked, "What do you think of this idea? Do you think it will work?"

When he said he liked my idea and thought it would work, I asked, "What do we need to do to make this happen?"

I processed the whole plan through him, and he jumped on board.

"Which would be the best way to propose this?" was my next question. "Should I bring it up, or is it something you'd like to do?"

This man is an initiator, and as I expected, he said, "Don't worry about it. I'll take care of it." He meant he would bring the matter to the board and become its chief advocate.

At the next board meeting, that influential person brought up the matter and used his well-earned influence to motivate the others. Because of their high level

According to George Barna, fifteen informal rules directed and defined youth of the mid to late 1990s. Now grown, those teens are emerging as leaders in our churches.

1. Personal relationships count. Institutions don't.
2. The process is more important than the product.
3. Aggressively pursue diversity among people.
4. Enjoying people and life opportunities is more important than productivity, profitability, or achievement.
5. Change is good.
6. The development of character is more crucial than achievement.
7. You can't always count on your family to be there for you, but it is your best hope for emotional support.
8. Each individual must assume responsibility for his or her own world.
9. Whenever necessary, gain control and use it wisely.
10. Don't waste time searching for absolutes. There are none.
11. One person can make a difference in the world, but not much.
12. Life is hard and then we die; but because it's the only life we have, we may as well endure it, enhance it, and enjoy it as best we can.
13. Spiritual truth may take many forms.
14. Express your rage.
15. Technology is our national ally.

George Barna, *Generation Next: What You Need to Know about Today's Youth* (Ventura, Calif.: Regal Books, 1993, 108–15)

of trust in this man, there was hardly any discussion. The measure passed with no dissent.

I wasn't trying to use (or misuse) the board member. If he had turned down my idea, I would not have persisted. Yet I knew that his influence would work far better than all the suggestions, pleas, and demands I might make.

Knowledge Is Power

At different times in history, people have perceived power differently. For example, a century ago in the Old West, a rancher showed power by counting heads of cattle. A decade ago, churches showed their influence and prestige by the number of buses in their parking lot. Our perceptions are changing. Although we've long been aware of the importance of knowledge, it is only within recent years that we have seen that knowledge (or information as it is sometimes called) is power.

We've always known that knowledge is power, of course, but it's truer than ever today. One thing leaders especially need to know, however, is that they don't have to know everything. When I was growing up, we lived by the unwritten law of the church that the pastor knew everything, the elders and deacons knew almost as much, and the people knew little. Not only did everyone assume that church leaders had to know everything; they also had to have the answers to every question, and they had to have at least two Bible verses to prove their point.

One of the most freeing experiences for any pastor is to say to the congregation, "I don't know." This becomes even more powerful when the same pastor says to elders and deacons, "Do you know what we should do? What's your opinion?" (This is just as true for leadership on every level. It's such a relief to students in Sunday school, for instance, when the teacher says, "I have no idea.")

To acknowledge ignorance not only frees pastors and other leaders from heavy burdens they can't carry, but it also frees them up to be human beings. In the process, people actually get to know them as fallible, and they can identify more readily with them as individuals. This confession invites others to share in the process of dealing with problematic situations.

We're living with what I call relational challenges. When we share information or allow others to share their information with us, we build bridges. We become vulnerable, but that's not the real issue. We enhance our authenticity and our credibility as we allow others to open up to us and we open up to them.

By contrast, imagine what it would be like in church if

- the organist or pianist discovered beautiful chords but didn't want to give the music away lest others play as well as he or she does.
- the youth pastor knew of a strategic influencer who had helped greatly to advance a certain program, but held that information so that no one else would know and take advantage of the same source.

Information Is Currency

In our world, information is the best currency. We barter information, and our information increases by sharing it. As soon as I give it away, I've increased it by giving it to someone else, who can then give it away and increase it even more. I'm not worried about who else is going to take that material and keep it.

It saddens me that pastors, elders, deacons, and teachers know things they don't pass on to their people. They would be more effective if they would share more.

One principle I apply to sharing information involves asking, "Who else needs to know this?" As soon as I begin to read a new piece of information that comes across my desk, I ask, "Who else can benefit from this?"

One of my roles as a Bible college president is to bring in funds for programs not covered by tuition. Most people would reason that we should keep our sources as secret as possible so that no one else would tap the same wallet or purse and thereby would cut off any future help for us. I don't believe that! In fact, once I share openly, the results amaze me. When I introduce my funders to somebody else who needs funding, we all become winners. This may not make sense to many people, but it works, and I've been advocating it for a long time. When someone comes to me needing money for a project I believe in, I point that person to someone who can help. Of course, there is the risk that Beulah Heights may lose some money, but so far that hasn't happened.

For instance, let's say Sara gives the college $10,000 annually because she believes in what we're doing. My friend Mark needs $6,000 for a project to work with the homeless, and I fully believe in what he's doing. What do I do? Do I tell Sara about him? If I do, she may fund him, leaving me with only $4,000 next year. Or even worse, she might just stop supporting Beulah Heights and give all her funds to Mark.

I've shared such information dozens of times, and I've never lost anything. For instance, I call Sara and tell her about Mark: "From some things you've said, I believe you have a heart for the homeless. Mark has a homeless shelter project that he's trying to start. May he talk to you?" Alternatively, I could say, "Okay, Mark, here's Sara's name and number. Call her and tell her I gave you the information." Every time I've done that, our funding has actually increased *from the same source.*

I've given away information and built a bridge, and everyone profited. Jesus laid down the principle: "If you give, you will receive. Your gift will return to you in full measure. . . . Whatever measure you use in giving—large or small—it will be used to measure what is given back to you" (Luke 6:38–39 NLT). Since Jesus set the example and gave the instructions I can give away sources and resources.

As a leader, I have chosen to work through people, so not only am I asking, "Who else can benefit from what I know?" but I'm also asking, "Who can help me?" Once I answer those questions, I am in the process of building a strategic team.

I don't have many committees at Beulah Heights, but I do have many ad hoc teams put together for a specific purpose. Once they have finished that task, they are dissolved. Sometimes I select the ad hoc team, and on other occasions, I ask the staff to do it.

Here's an example I gleaned from the book *Lexus and the Olive Tree: Understanding Globalization* (New York: Anchor Books, 2000) by Thomas Friedman. He writes about core values in a globalized or interrelated world. His book prompted an idea that I began to use at the college, and it works wonderfully.

We wanted to discover our top five core values at the institution, things that will never change about us and that help define who we are as BHBC. Because I didn't want to choose a team strictly from my frame of reference, I called a staff meeting and said, "Pretend that Beulah Heights Bible College has been invited to open an extension on Mars, and there's a rocket ship leaving for that planet next week. It only holds enough room for seven people. On the paper in front of you, write the names of the seven people you would nominate to ride on the rocket ship—people who would best represent us. There are only two rules. First, you may not nominate yourself. Second, you may not nominate me."

When I collected the "ballots," we had a total of eighty names. My assistant, Jackie Armstrong, put the names on a grid of those nominated most often and calculated them until we came up with the seven most-nominated names. The person with the most nominations was Benson Karanja, an African. The person with the second highest was Robert Melson, who had been on staff for only three months.

Once the team came together, I asked them to work out the core values that would guide them in starting the extension school on Mars. They worked on that and took their decisions to the entire staff. The others listened, interacted, made suggestions, and then the team went back to work. Four times the ad hoc team went to the entire group, but eventually we knew our core values.

Innovation Is Success

Innovation answers the question, "What can we do that nobody else is doing?" That is a very difficult and courageous question to ask.

Our first discovery was the need for training in urban ministry. No other Bible college was doing urban ministry. Even now we're the only accredited Bible college in the southern United States that offers an undergraduate major in urban ministry. Since many of our people will never go on to graduate school, we saw a need to provide a major at the undergraduate level.

In the fall of 2000, we began another major that we called Leadership. As far as I know, this course is one of a kind in the United States. We don't call it "Church Leadership," "Pastoral Leadership," "Ministry Leadership," or "Personal Leadership." Our mission is to train every type of leader for the marketplace as well as for service in the church. No one else was providing a leadership or urban ministry major when we started those two programs. That's what we mean by innovation.

Those grappling with the issues of the futuring church must look carefully at their demographics and use that information to determine what kind of services or ministries they need to offer and the kind of people they need to staff them.

Furthermore, they must determine what skills people need for new services or ministries. For example, if I had been a youth leader five years ago and my competency hadn't increased, I wouldn't be able to relate effectively to today's youth. Yet I find too many still focusing on the traditional methods of the past. They promote youth camp, VBS, and youth rallies—and none of those things are wrong or bad; they're just a bit outdated. Innovative programs are more family oriented, and activities are scheduled only for evening hours.

Beulah Heights planned an innovative activity for young people in our community who had no direct contact with BHBC. We received private funding to take thirty kids and ten chaperones to Sea World in Orlando, Florida, to a Monday-to-Friday leadership-training conference. These were all inner-city kids who had never been outside the projects, and they came from seventeen different churches.

We had the money for expenses, but the one thing we didn't have was transportation. One day I spoke about plans to go to Orlando with a warm, caring Christian friend named Don Chapman.

"How are you going to get the kids from Atlanta to Orlando?" he asked.

"By bus," I said. "We haven't made the reservations yet—that's the one thing we'll work on next week. We've decided that we'll probably charter a bus."

"No, don't do that. Fly them," he said.

"But we don't have enough money to do that," I replied.

"I'm on the board for AirTran. Just write me a note that explains what you want to do, and I'll take care of it." It was just that simple as far as Don was concerned.

That same day I wrote to him and asked if he could arrange for an airplane to take thirty kids and ten chaperones on a certain date and bring them back.

Gary McIntosh once led a workshop that discussed "That Was Then vs. This Is Now." The table below lists some of the observations that came from that workshop.

That Was Then	This Is Now
More structure driven	More mission driven
People served out of duty and obligation	People serve out of passion and gifting
More leader dependent	Greater shared responsibility
More top-down authority and information	Teams get input from everyone
Power and control	Empowerment of the team
Teams focused on task or relationship	Focuses on both
Leadership was assigned or transferred	Leadership emerges

Don was as good as his word. AirTran flew our kids both ways without the kids or Beulah Heights paying a cent. And once in Orlando, fresh creative lessons at Sea World provided a hands-on learning situation for the kids.

Beulah Heights didn't receive any direct benefit, and neither did I. That wasn't our purpose. The kids benefited and learned—that was our purpose. This is an example of the church finding its place in the community in new ways. We must offer more than just a Sunday morning service that includes praise and worship, an offering, and a sermon. Instead, we need to offer innovative ministries that meet the needs of the people.

Here's something else. Small groups have changed. It used to be that we set up small groups/cell groups/home groups by zip codes. Now we establish groups by interests. For example, one group of teens may want to play basketball, another may want to go fishing, another golfing, and yet another walking around the mall.

I visited a church that offered five-week courses on gourmet cooking, landscaping, small business start-up, and art instruction. The classes were packed, and many who attended were not church members.

I like to think of these kinds of programs as innovation in the midst of tradition. Churches that innovate move along with speed. They don't bog down new ideas by referring them to feasibility committees. They don't get overwhelmed and discouraged because a few Christians ask every time they present a new idea, "What are we going to get out of this?"

I remember a white church in the 1970s that had a lovely playground. The area began to change, and blacks moved in. A deacon appointed himself to make sure that none of those nonchurch kids played inside the fenced-in grounds. As he did that, the pastor visited newcomers to the community.

"You mean we can come and sit in your pews, but our kids can't play on your swings?" one father asked.

The pastor changed the policy, but by then it was too late. The new arrivals to the community had already figured the church didn't want them. The deacon continued to speak against the reversal of policy. "We paid for these swings. I spent many Saturday afternoons getting this playground ready. What do we get out of letting those kids play here?"

He never did get the point, because his focus was only on what the local church would receive for their investment.

But, as Christians, we are called to serve others. Therefore, as leaders, we have to help people like this deacon change their thinking. Instead of ignoring their questions, because they ask out of their sense of need and their understanding of the gospel, we should try what I call oblique thinking.

> Futuring leaders realize that if they are going to grow and take others forward, they can never stop learning. They know that knowledge is power, and they are learning to barter with it. They increase information by sharing knowledge. And through innovation, they move into new areas and successfully proclaim the message of God's love.

Oblique thinking would say to those who ask such questions, "You know, there may be some truth in that." Then we need to follow up with our own question: "How do we bridge the gap? How do we manifest the love of Jesus Christ and serve others?"

I've suggested to several congregational leaders that they approach the situation differently. That gets away from asking, "What do we get out of this?" They begin by sending money to support a homeless shelter. Get people in the church to think about such places and pray for the ministry to the homeless. After a period of time, designate a day once a month when members of the congregation visit the shelter to serve people food, talk with them, and wash dishes.

A similar ministry is sponsored by the youth of a church thirty miles north of Atlanta. They go to an inner-city church that houses the homeless each night. Twenty-two teens and four leaders meet at 5:30 A.M. on Sunday and drive to a shelter the church has supported for five years. They bring all the necessary food and prepare breakfast, then clean up afterward. That's only one congregation. Many others are doing similar ministries in cities across the country.

When we engage in these projects, we may never receive even one new member. It's not likely that the homeless people will come and worship with us. But even when we don't see measurable results, we have followed the example of Jesus, reached out with compassion, and shown kindness and caring.

ELEVEN

Creative Leadership

The eighth trait of futuring leaders is creative leadership. The word *creativity* may scare some. It means thinking outside the box and coloring outside the lines. It means daring to look around and envision what lies ahead. And it means questioning the old ways and asking, "Is there a newer, more efficient method?" Most futuring leaders do this instinctively, but all of us can also learn to think creatively.

Thinking creatively is one of futuring leaders' primary responsibilities. For things to happen, they have to dream and see the impossible as within their grasp. But too often the people who most need to think creatively lock themselves into one style of thinking. Instead, they need to incorporate three kinds of thinking—*strategic, genius,* and *oblique.*

> Many churches are stuck. They provide programs instead of experiences.

Strategic Thinking

Strategic thinking is another name for logical or analytic thinking. We are at point A, and we want to reach point B and then move to C and on to D. This kind of visioning asks basic questions that can't be avoided:

> Creativity at work: The American space program spent millions of dollars to develop a pen that could write in zero gravity. The Soviets used pencils.

Who is going to do it?

When will it get done?

How much is it going to cost?

Who is going to be accountable for this project?

What are the marks of success and failure?

How do we evaluate the success or failure of the venture?

How do we know that we want to move from B to C? Do we stay at B? Should we skip C and go to D?

Genius Thinking

Genius thinking goes beyond strategic thinking. It begins by recognizing the available resources but it also recognizes that the resources are limited.

Strategic thinking says, "This is what we have to work with, and this is what we are going to do. This is the amount of money we need, the number of people involved, and the building we require." The plan is laid out logically. Genius thinking starts at this point and seeks possibilities that others haven't considered. I like to think of it this way: The difference between a leader and a manager is that managers work with or "manage" resources that are given to them by leaders.

Leaders say, "We need more space and more workers. Now let's see what we can do to get more." They search for creative ways to resource themselves. This isn't to say that we don't need managers—we do—but we need leaders first and managers to come in behind and support them. No one should say that a leader is more important than a manager. If

> Leadership isn't about resources; it's about resourcefulness.

someone were to ask me which is more important, I'd have to respond with my own question: "What wing of the airplane is more important to keep it flying? The left or the right?"

Leaders	Managers
Emphasize *what* and *why*	Emphasize *how* and *when*
Work from the future back to the present	Work from the past to the present
Focus on the long term	Focus on the short term or immediate
Embrace a macro-perspective	Embrace a micro-perspective
Favor innovative thinking	Favor routine/safe thinking
Seek to balance idealism with realism	Emphasize pragmatism over idealism
Show revolutionary flair	Protect status quo
Clarify the vision	Implement the vision
Inspire and motivate	Control and direct
Excite others by change	Are threatened by change
Decide quickly	Decide slowly
Identify opportunities	Identify obstacles
Take risks	Avoid risks
Pursue resources	Actions limited to available resources
People centered	System centered
Idea centered	Plan centered
Centered on core issues	Distracted by peripheral issues
Want others' approval	Need others' approval
Do the right thing	Do things right

For us in the futuring church, growth management is a tremendous challenge. Genius thinking sees possibilities and says, "We can make that happen." Too often

Observations about Leaders and Managers

- Leaders and managers complement each other.
- Both need to work in the area of their strengths.
- Successful managers aren't always successful leaders; successful leaders aren't necessarily successful managers.
- We need to evaluate the success of managers differently from the success of leaders.
- We consider managers successful when they operate the organization efficiently as well as deliver services on time and within budget.
- We consider leaders successful when they enable their organization to grow in its ability to serve the community by discovering new needs, expanding the resources base, and innovating approaches to service delivery, and when they energize or transform the organization.

native thinking says, "Let's send it to a committee for recommendations."

Genius thinking also rephrases concepts. For example, although this isn't original with BHBC, on our campus we don't use the word *problems.* We prefer the word *challenge.* By changing our use of just one word, we present a different picture in people's minds. *Problems* easily lead to dead ends or at least to a lot of struggling. *Challenges* give us opportunities to overcome hindrances.

> The right people in the right place create a winning team.

Another sentence, again not original, that my staff uses often is "The difficult we do at once, the impossible takes a little longer." This challenges them not to throw up their hands and roll their eyes but to say, "We don't know what to do—yet."

Oblique Thinking

Oblique thinking looks for options that are neither white nor black. Most of the time, people think in terms of either/or when they could be thinking both/and. Let's see how this works in a growing church that we'll call Bethel Gospel Church.

The pastor asks, "Do we continue to grow so that we build a bigger congregation? Or should we plant another church?"

That question implies a lack of oblique thinking. Why couldn't they have both? That is, why can't they have *two* growing churches?

There was a time when churches decided to relocate that one of the first things leaders said was "We need to sell this present building before we can build another." Oblique thinking says, "This is a transitional community, and we need to relocate. That's obvious. For us to relocate, do we have to sell this present building?"

The answer is "No, we don't have to sell." Oblique thinking asks, "Why can't we use the present facilities as a mission base? Why can't we become part of another church that is already in this area? Why can't we resource them?"

Another innovation that is a result of oblique thinking is that we see shared facilities all over the country. One building may house congregations that hold services in English, Korean, and Spanish.

Why would we want to construct a building and invest at least a million dollars for cathedral ceilings and ornate glass windows for only two and a half hours a week? Is that good stewardship? Instead, oblique thinking asks, "What else can this money be used for?"

For example, I visited a large Midwestern church with theater-style, pushback seating for 3,500 with additional seating in the balcony. The church has only one service

> Creativity is a futuring leader's primary responsibility and involves three kinds of thinking: *strategic*, *genius*, and *oblique*.

that begins at 10:30 and ends ninety minutes later. That ninety minutes is the only time the congregation uses the auditorium. The rest of the time they rent the facility to civic groups, orchestras, schools, and fund-raising groups. Not only is that oblique thinking, but they're also serving their community. While they are meeting the needs of their people and the community, their multimillion-dollar building isn't standing vacant six days a week.

We must always keep asking ourselves, "What else can we do?" When we think in that way, we are more aware of the needs of others. We consider what we can do to help people outside the church so that together we can break down the walls that divide us.

Someone once said, "The greatest pleasure in life is doing what people think can't be done." I do know that creativity can make things happen that no one thought about before.

TWELVE

Timing

The ninth trait of futuring leadership is timing. The past is prologue, the present is action now, and the future shows the results of our present decisions. All of this is *par* for the course.

Prologue. The past provides background and reminds us of where we've been. No matter how much we remember, we cannot change or improve the past.

Action takes place in the present, but we direct those decisions toward the future.

Results refer totally to the future, because we can't foresee the outcome when we make our decisions.

The space between the past and the future closes almost instantly. By that I mean that we're always living and working in the future. We're never in the past. Most of us are barely in the present. As soon as we blink, we're into the future that we thought about only minutes ago.

Three Practical Truths

Charles Moeller Jr. noted that leaders in growing churches know, understand, and apply what he calls three practical axioms or self-evident truths.

1. "The past is a foreign country; they do things differently there." This offers a handle on understanding and applying lessons from the past.
2. "There are no future decisions, only present decisions with future consequences." This helps to meaningfully connect today and tomorrow.
3. "Most of today's problems were yesterday's solutions." This helps us slow down in moments of decision making.

As we think about timing, it helps if we make this a motto of our thinking: The past is prologue. That is, when we look backward, we gain insight into the background, the reasons for particular actions, and the needs that brought about such decisions.

The past is over. We can do nothing to improve the past. Obviously, our actions must take place in the present. But that's not enough, because our actions must be grounded in the future. That is, actions taken right now can't simply be for the matter of expediency or to get rid of a pressing challenge. Whatever decisions and choices we make will have implications for and results in the future, and we need to be aware of what they will be.

That is especially significant when we talk about long-range planning. I smile as I think about the term *long-range planning*. During my college days and into my pastoral years, we constantly heard about looking far ahead and making plans for the next decade. We thought in large blocks of at least five years and often projected that to ten or fifteen or even twenty. That's outmoded and impossible today because of the rapidity of change in our world. Today the outer limits on long-range planning are three years—and even that may be too far ahead and need corrections.

Fast-moving, rapidly growing churches do what they call "annual planning"—but they do the planning at *quarterly* meetings. Is it any wonder they're growing? They're staring into the immediate future. They also incorporate preparedness, an even better concept than long-range planning. Their goal is to be ready *now* for what happens next week or anywhere up ahead.

One way to see how futuring works is to look at the concept from the historical context of the last century. In the 1930s, France's minister of war oversaw the construction of a complex system of fortifications along its eastern border from Switzerland to Belgium. France built antitank barriers of upright rail sections embedded in concrete in front of it. They also constructed an underground fortress that housed twelve hundred men. They referred to it as the Maginot Line, named after André Maginot, who saw the permanent barrier as the most practical way to protect the regions of Alsace and Lorraine against a surprise German attack.

This extensive plan gave the French a false security and an undue reliance on static defense that has since been called the "Maginot mentality." Too late the French realized the ineffectiveness of their long-range planning when the German army circumvented the barrier and entered France through Belgium at the start of World War II. The French had made long-range plans and carried them through, but unfortunately, the style of warfare changed drastically between the two world wars.

Being prepared for the future is more important than planning for it. If an opportunity comes to us today, we must be ready—right now—to move on it. Decisions that used to go to committees and then subcommittees and sometimes feasibility groups sometimes took three years before being finalized. Life isn't waiting that long today.

Let's suppose I'm a pastor in a growing church and our present facilities are filled to capacity. From a realtor friend, I learn about a piece of land that is on the market today. It's valuable and it's in the perfect location.

"This land won't stay available," he says. "I've already had three other calls." Because he's my friend, he says, "Here's what I'll do. I'll hold this property until 3:00 this afternoon. If I don't receive a bid from you by then, don't bother to call me later."

What do I do? What can I do? Do I, as a pastor, have the power to act? Is there someone I can call who has the authority to act? Must I wait to call a board meeting and then appoint a committee?

Too late! The land is already gone.

If our church is in a state of preparation, we can act. If we're still doing long-range planning, we probably aren't even aware that we'll need to buy new land.

We can learn from the business world. Mergers and buyouts happen so quickly that it's nearly impossible to keep up with them. I was in Davenport, Iowa, in the summer of 2001. Two years earlier, I had driven by the Oscar Mayer processing plant. When I drove by this time, the buildings were the same, but the sign now said, "Kraft." It was still producing Oscar Mayer products, but was owned by Kraft. I was in the city for two days, and I asked at least eight people, "When did Kraft buy Oscar Mayer?"

"Did they do that?" was the usual answer. One of them knew the business had changed hands, but had no idea when it had happened.

That's the way our world operates today. Everything rushes down the fast track.

Since the advent of the wind-up clock (1876) and the battery-operated watch (1956), there has been a shift from living in high touch time to high tech time. In contrast to the language of high touch time, phrases today reveal a sense of urgency about time: lack of time, quick time, real time, face time, deadline, checklist, multitask, behind, finding time, making time, losing time, filling time, killing time, spending time, wasting time, on time out of time, time frame, fast-forward.

John Naisbitt, Nana Naisbitt, and Douglas Philips, *High Tech High Touch: Technology and Our Search for Meaning* (New York: Broadway Books, 1999, 33)

Let's go back to the challenge of available land. A futuring church would have foreseen the need for larger facilities at least a year in advance of the land's availability. They would already have been watching and waiting for the right piece of real estate to go on the market. And because they were prepared, they would have empowered someone to act immediately.

This scenario played out in real life for Bishop Eddie Long's church, New Birth Missionary Baptist, a church with an average weekly attendance of eighteen thousand. He was told about a prime piece of real estate a considerable distance from his church. It was undeveloped and had no light or water facilities.

New Birth bought the property, not to use for themselves, but to make a profit. Fourteen months later, New Birth sold the property and made five million dollars for the congregation. That meant that when they moved into their new building—on which they had already started construction—they were able to hold their first services in a multimillion-dollar building that was already debt free. That's futuring!

Bishop Long is one of many dynamic futuring leaders. He looks at what is and envisions what can be. Then he acts. He and other visionaries are prepared for the future today.

Planning Ahead

What we see now has value. It has the same value as my rearview and sideview mirrors, which tell me where I've been and if something is coming up behind me. But we can't drive with our eyes focused on what we've already passed. We keep thinking we can look backward and see how it was done once and then adapt it for the future. That just doesn't work.

Let's say I live in an area that is rapidly transitioning from a single-home community into an apartment community. That's the future, so everything I do now has to interface with that reality.

> One thing we learn from history is that we don't learn from history.
>
> Winston Churchill

If I know that my community is getting younger because families with small children are moving in, I also realize that our church has an opportunity to gain more young families. To make that happen, our church will need a playground for those children as well as a well-equipped nursery and staff. We also will need to ask ourselves, "What else can we offer that will attract these new families?"

As far as I'm concerned, the most vital places in and around the church—beginning with their order of importance—are:

First, the nursery.
Second, the ladies' room.
Third, the foyer.

Fourth, the parking lot.

Fifth, the sanctuary.

This order may surprise some. One person challenged me on the foyer as third. It is, however, the place where members have fellowship and build relationships. It's where small talk opens the way for more significant talk later. If we have a narrow, small, dark, or dingy foyer, it's functional—like a cattle chute. But people don't want to talk in a crowded hallway where they are constantly being bumped. If we provide a larger, well-lit space as a foyer, people are more likely to congregate and chat with each other.

Since we're looking at the future to see the kind of people who will attend our church, suppose we consider the needs of the growing senior population. How will our facilities fit their needs?

I know a church in the Midwest that was built in the 1960s when most of the members were in their thirties and had young children. They outgrew their small building and built a larger one. When people entered the front door of the new building, they had two choices. They could walk up a flight of stairs to the sanctuary, or they could walk down the stairs to the restrooms and educational facilities.

That was fine in 1960, but flash forward forty years. The building doesn't suit the needs of the current members, and the church is dying. Few of those thirty-something people who are still alive go there. "I can't climb the stairs," one woman said with tears in her eyes. "I can't even go to my own church anymore."

Five of her lifelong friends have also stopped going to church. They say "We're too old to search for a new church, and we can't walk up the stairs at our own."

Oh, yes, the church leadership is aware of the situation. They have been studying the problem for almost four years.

Have I made my point?

Modern church planning requires serious architectural study, and a key consideration is space for expansion. Thus, most new church development is being done in three phases. First, they construct the building for worship; then they expand the auditorium; and finally, they erect a balcony—something that went out of fashion two generations ago and is now making a comeback. Many new church buildings are being constructed with high ceilings so that a balcony can be added if necessary.

Practical Planning

Suppose I walked into a room with ten pastors present and asked, "What will your church look like ten years from now?"

I don't think many of them would know. I don't know either, but I could help them, because I know where they do their best thinking. It starts with what happened in the past. I've done this many times, and the results are about the same on each occasion.

I ask them to take out two sheets of paper and I say, "On the first page, I want you to list ten major changes that have taken place within the past decade of your ministry." I wait and they write. Within a few minutes, they've completed that list, because it's easy to write.

Then I say, "Using that material to help you do your thinking, on the second page, write a list of changes you foresee within the next five years."

They stare at me. Sometimes they leave the page blank. They may scribble a few words, but few of them know how to answer the question.

My point is this: Too many church leaders spend most of their time fixing the past and managing the present, so they can't make time to prepare for the future.

Remember, the past is prologue, the present is action, and the future is results. This forms an acrostic:

Prologue—the past is done. And no one can improve it.

Action takes place in the present. But it points toward the future.

Results are in the future and reveal what will be achieved.

All of this is par for the course.

We have discussed nine significant characteristics that futuring leaders need to develop. In chapter 13, we will discover one more powerful element they need to incorporate. They need to look ahead, peek over the horizon, and be ready for what lies ahead.

THIRTEEN

Future Gazing

The tenth trait of futuring leadership is future gazing.

Futuring church leaders forecast trends, envision scenarios, and help to create the desired future. To reach that desired future, we have to shift our thinking. We can no longer stumble along and trust that somehow the Spirit of God will intervene and lead us into the Promised Land of excitement and spiritual growth.

The Bible is quite clear that God gives the growth, but it also tells us that God uses people to prepare the fields and plant the seed. When we have done what we can, then God does indeed give the increase and also completes the tasks that we, as humans, can't do. Paul says it this way: "I planted the seed, Apollos watered it, but God made it grow" (1 Cor. 3:6).

Well-known writer Henry Blackaby has encouraged us to ask the all-important question, "Where are you going, God?" Then we go where God is going instead of inviting him to go along with our plans.

Successful futuring churches don't just happen, even though God sometimes blesses in spite of our ignorance or lack of planning. Doesn't it make sense to follow God's way—to seek God's guidance each step of the way?

As I've been stressing all through this book, if we want to give ourselves the highest possibilities not just for survival but also for growth, we need leaders who prepare for the future.

That makes staffing a primary issue. We used to work on a simple system. We had a solo pastor. Then as the church grew, we hired an assistant to take over the youth work; or in some churches, the second staff person did educational work. If the congregation continued to grow, we hired another person to do specialized ministry. We had paid choir directors, organists, and pianists. That's what we needed in 1930, and we still needed them in 1980. What do we need now?

> Church champions need to help church leaders develop and sustain new models of eliminating biblical illiteracy in spiritual life.
>
> George W. Bullard Jr.
> *LN BookNotes*,
> July 2000

Instead of opting for a young minister or assistant pastor, futuring churches hire a person they call by various terms, such as "spiritual development director," to be responsible for developing spirituality within the congregation. And some churches no longer hire choir directors. That's too narrow a focus. Instead, they seek someone who can incorporate music, dance, and drama in worship services.

Futuring leaders have recognized that it's not enough to minister to the youth; they need to find ways to impact the parents and other family members. Therefore, they hire those who can establish and teach family foundations by working with entire families.

Another characteristic of growing churches is that they now have executive or administration pastors, although the term may not always be used. These pastors deal only with the administrative responsibilities of the congregation. A church doesn't call such pastors to preach or teach

> Futuring church leaders forecast trends, envision scenarios, and help to create the desired future.

but to do administrative work, because that's their gift. They take care of the business of the church, such as staffing, budgeting, and other routine matters.

At a church leadership conference, Leonard Sweet said that we no longer live in the land of the status quo; we live in the land of status flux. He called it a seascape, because, unlike the landscape where our feet rest on solid ground and we can predict future events, we live in what he calls an "aquaculture" where everything is in constant change.

I've spelled out ten characteristics of futuring leaders. In the next chapter, I look at the trends we need to face that remind us, "This ain't your daddy's church." Although our foundation is secure in Jesus Christ, the struggles we face are new. To be aware of these trends is to begin seeking ways of coping with them.

FOURTEEN

Forty-four Trends*

Church leaders have spotted some trends in American churches that we believe will continue. Some are further along than others, but within five years these changes probably will have occurred. Some are happening in mainline denominations, and most are emerging among independent congregations. Regardless, they are happening—now.

I'm listing these trends because congregations need to take action on them. We can't act on or react to anything we don't know about. As you read this chapter, my hope is that your thinking will become more flexible and you will consider ways to respond to these challenges.

To get this picture more clearly, let's try to imagine ourselves going to sleep in 1963 and waking up in 2003. We walk up to a church deacon and ask, "What has changed?"

*I do not advocate, endorse, or encourage the trends discussed in this chapter. They will, however, serve as catalysts for futuring.

Forty-four Trends in Churches Today

1. Denominations are not an issue.
2. The term *home church* has no relevance.
3. Cell churches (we used to call them home groups or neighborhood Bible studies) are changing.
4. People are involved in the church without attending each Sunday.
5. High spirituality and low organized religion mark futuring church congregations.
6. Worship service days and times vary.
7. Worship structures are changing.
8. Worship styles are changing.
9. Evangelism takes place in both seeker-sensitive as well as more blatant forms.
10. Revival comes in different forms.
11. The church develops rather than trains.
12. Education for the church is moving from teaching to learning.
13. Leadership teams replace single leaders.
14. Decisions are made by consensus.
15. Church governments are changing.
16. The church is being forced to rethink sexuality.
17. The demand for excellence increases.
18. Church leaders are being held to stricter requirements.
19. Immigrants seek a vision- and purpose-driven church.
20. Discipline in the church is expected and implemented.
21. Relevancy is in demand.
22. Immigrants stress effectiveness and measurable benchmarks.

"Everything has changed," he answers.

"Yes, but specifically, what has changed?"

He tells us about advances in technology and transportation, changes in the family structure, how houses are now being built and where they're located. He talks about cell phones, the commute structure, and the entertainment industry. The list becomes almost endless.

23. Family time is a premium consideration.
24. Pastoral care has higher demands.
25. Future churches recognize and respond to single-parent homes.
26. The number of younger retirees continues to grow.
27. America is getting grayer.
28. We have the mall motif—everything under one roof.
29. Multimedia will be an increasing reality.
30. Technology—e-mail, connecting people—will have major implications for how we do ministry, especially in global missions.
31. Consumerism has come to church.
32. Money is now plentiful.
33. Financial accountability is a must.
34. Urbanization or cross-cultural shifts are becoming the rule.
35. The concept of missions is changing.
36. Social action is receiving a strong emphasis—especially partnership with government programs.
37. Futuring churches are increasingly active in local politics.
38. Church and state issues change.
39. Shared church facilities will increase.
40. The doctrine of tolerance remains an immense challenge to the health of the church.
41. The church is suffering and will suffer persecution.
42. Cult activity and satanic powers continue to have a great influence on our world.
43. Both false prophets and true prophets are emerging.
44. Future churches live and flourish with contradictions.

Here's the tragedy in this scenario: Most of our churches went to sleep decades ago. Even though they appear to be awake, they're oblivious to changes that have taken place in the culture that affect the church. I can say that without hesitation because I've visited hundreds of congregations since the beginning of the new millennium that show no significant changes in their worship experiences over the past forty years.

The good news is that churches are waking up—and part of the reason for that awakening is that we're being forced to shake ourselves and go through serious self-examination. The tendency, of course, is to want to return to the way things were before. If we open our eyes wide, like Rip Van Winkle did after he had slept for twenty years, and return to our village, we're faced with a shocking reality: Nothing has remained the same. Like Van Winkle, we're tempted to throw our energy into making time go backward, but it's impossible.

That's the tension we face today. We long for the simpler ways and the clear-cut choices between right and wrong. "In the good old days," we had few questions about morals and the role of authority figures. Now we have to shift our thinking. Tensions increase as we examine the wide gap between what things used to be, what they have become, and what the gap will be in another decade.

It's a shame that we haven't been sensitive to the prompting of the Holy Spirit so that we could become the change leaders in the world. In fact, it's the reverse. Serious transformations in society are forcing the awakening church to reexamine itself. And we tend to scream, groan, and grumble the whole time.

The forty-four trends are listed in random order because I'm not sure of their importance. In various parts of the country, believers will see one issue as having higher priority than other areas—that's another drastic shift from forty-plus years ago.

1. *Denominations are not an issue.* There was a time when, if Baptists moved to Seattle from Chicago and were in search of a new church, they considered *only* Baptist churches. That is no longer true. The same held true for Presbyterians, Methodists, and independents. This trend of putting less importance on denominations has been going on for at least twenty-five years, but it

is becoming important enough that denominational leaders are studying it seriously.

Many people prefer a *style* of worship, and the denominational tag means little. If we drive by newer church structures, we find an interesting phenomenon. Fifty years ago the denomination name stood out in large letters. Today some churches are putting their denominational affiliation on their signs in small letters or leaving it off all together. Immigrants may visit a church and not even realize they're in a Missouri Synod Lutheran or Pentecostal Holiness church.

When natives move, they still seek "our church." Immigrants, however, don't look for the closest Methodist church, although they're not averse to joining one. They're more caught up in pragmatic issues:

- How convenient is it to get there?
- How many miles is it from our house?
- What services do they offer?
- Do they have family programs and youth activities?

Perhaps unconsciously immigrants seek a particular leadership style. They may not be able to define it, but they recognize it when they find it. They seek interaction that will be available to them *at their choosing.* They may choose not to be heavily involved, and they don't want to attend a congregation where they're made to feel guilty for not subscribing to all the tenets of the church. They want to hold many options.

The basic beliefs, such as the statement of faith, may still be important, but the form of worship, style of ministry, and the warmth (or lack of it) among members take preeminence over theological issues.

Virtually unheard of a few years ago, today thousands of Christians will go to another denomination's church

I sat next to a godly Christian leader at a funeral. He has an out-standing ministry of helping congregations raise funds for new building projects. As we waited for the service to start, he leaned over and said, "You know, Sam, with my travel schedule, I'm rarely at church at my home church. I'm in a church every Sunday and often in midweek worship but rarely at my home church." He thought about it and said, "At most, I'm among my home congregation once a month, and I have no opportunities to serve. I feel I have so much to offer, because I'm around more churches and I know the issues they're facing and can see challenges that lie ahead.

"You know something sad?" he asked and sighed. "I can never become a leader in my own church. To move into any leadership role, we must attend every Sunday unless we're on vacation. How are people like me who have so much to offer plugged into the leadership of the church? My church has so much to gain from my experience, but I'm invisible there."

I wish I had been able to give him an answer.

that doesn't subscribe to all the tenets they have been used to. Check out any growing congregation and ask how many are natives to that denomination. It's amazing how few are. It's equally amazing how many have come from a variety of other backgrounds.

Immigrants know that life involves trade-offs. No one church can offer them everything they want. They know they'll never have all they are looking for. So if the church they visit has a good program for their children, they are willing to make trade-offs—and the theological differences seem less important than the care of their children.

2. *The term* home church *has no relevance.* Natives thought of exclusive and long-term membership in one congregation. Immigrants are shoppers for the faith, and they seek short-term relationships with several congregations.

There was a time when we'd meet other Christians and one of the first questions we would ask was, "What's your home church?" We could use that to label them— not in a negative sense. When we heard the answer, we knew how to respond and how to direct the conversation from there. It was a useful get-acquainted device.

Today that question is increasingly unlikely to provide answers. Because immigrants have become shoppers for the faith, they don't feel tied down with long-term relationships with a single congregation. Natives are aghast, but immigrants have not bought into the idea of church loyalty. In fact, many immigrants join with a congregation assuming they will experience a short-term relationship.

Typically, natives stress *duty*. They feel an obligation to stay in one church. They teach a Sunday school class year after year. Or they volunteer to help in the nursery, and fifteen years later, they're still there. Natives were raised in a society where *duty* and *obligation* were key culture words.

Today, duty is dead and obligation is unemployed. How does the futuring church get around this trend? The old method was for those in the pulpit to induce guilt. When natives considered leaving, leaders preached and taught to make them struggle with questions such as, "What will people think?" and "Will we be failing God if we stop ushering every Sunday?" Because of the short-term mind-set, guilt doesn't work anymore. Immigrants have multiple needs, and our culture encourages them to be service driven, getting what they can from different places. They might go to one church on Wednesday nights because that church has an excellent program for their teens. On Sunday morning they attend another church as a family because they like the outstanding choir or the powerful preaching. They also might enroll in small groups and be with people they don't attend church with.

Years ago many churches developed the idea of cell groups or neighborhood gatherings to keep their members focused on the church. That's not the way it works today. Immigrants may become regular members of a cell group only because it meets a specific need they have.

What about Christian leaders whose responsibilities don't allow them to worship at their church regularly? Can they have a purpose and function in that church? In my own case, I'm certain to be at my home church on Easter, Mother's Day, and Christmas but not on many other Sundays.

3. *Cell churches (we used to call them home groups or neighborhood Bible studies) are changing.* Because people in our society have become so disconnected from one another, there is an even greater inner need to be connected. That disconnection has highlighted the need for community. Immigrants want to be attached to small groups, so growing larger churches break their members down into smaller groups. The purpose of small groups isn't to grow a church, but to grow the person.

Previously, churches divided home groups by zip codes and neighborhoods because they focused on the convenience of driving or walking within the neighborhood. Geographic convenience no longer holds the appeal. Instead, the trend is to emphasize age and areas of interest, such as Bible study, music, golfing, fishing, shopping, and parenting.

The old cell groups used to be Bible-study based. The trend is now toward relationships. Is the Bible involved? Yes. Do they have Bible studies? Yes, they do—but they're different. If immigrants get together for two hours twice a month, they may spend fifteen or twenty minutes in structured Bible study. The rest of the time is directional or applicational, and especially they seek guidance on ethical issues.

"What does the Bible say about nuclear war?"

"Our daughter wants her boyfriend to live with her in our house. What do I do?"

"How are we supposed to relate to our Muslim neighbors?" These are real-life struggles and challenges.

Today's church members want to talk about their families, challenges they face in the workplace, events in their lives, and transitions they're involved in.

"Is there somebody else out there who's going through what I'm going through? If so, can we talk about it?" may be the approach.

Thus, the essence of the cell group has changed from church based and Bible study based, to relationship based and affinity group based.

4. *People are involved in the church without attending each Sunday.* Growing churches will have people who are serious about their level of spirituality but without a Sunday-go-to-meeting attitude. Their concern is "How do I live my faith during the week? How do I apply what I'm learning?"

The relationship between serving God and attending church every Sunday doesn't mean the same to immigrants as it does for natives. Immigrants are strong about living out their spirituality, but they don't think they have to be in church every week to do that.

Immigrants see their spiritual lives like this: One day they're fully involved at Grace Assembly. They may not be sitting in church the next week, but it doesn't mean they're not serving the Lord. It simply means that the relationship between serving God and attending church every Sunday doesn't hold the same meaning for immigrants that it does for natives.

For us natives, something was wrong if we didn't attend church at least three out of four Sundays each

month. People just didn't consider us spiritual or committed to Christ.

5. *High spirituality and low organized religion mark
futuring church congregations.* Natives were taught to
live their spirituality through the opportunities for service within their own congregation. Modern spirituality is lived out Monday through Sunday and much of
that outside the context of organized religion or through
parachurch, faith-based community outreach.

If immigrants want to disinfect mattresses at a homeless shelter, they'll do it even if it's not on their church's
to-do list. They might choose to become involved in programs sponsored by their local church, but they're not
limited to them.

In the past, organized religion would say, "Come to
church. Be involved in our programs. This is what we offer
and what's going on." Spirituality was lived out through
the worship experience or opportunities for service.

Spirituality is now being lived out at a different level.
Immigrants consider it a higher level, because they live
their faith Monday through Sunday and do most of it
outside the context of organized religion or beyond the
walls of a single church. Natives, however, have limited
themselves to saying, "Our church does this. These are
the programs we're involved in."

6. *Worship service days and times vary.* The two fastest-
growing types of churches in America are those that
have church services that begin no later than 8:30 Sunday morning (some as early as 7:30) and those that offer
worship on Friday or Saturday evening.

In fact, Friday or Saturday evening services attract
more of the unreached. Christians can invite others
much more easily. "Let's go to church tonight. It'll start
at 6:30, and we'll be out by 8:00. Why don't our families
get together for dinner after that?" This fits the immigrant lifestyle, because they don't want to tie up their

entire weekend for a church service. This way they can go in, worship, and have the rest of the weekend free.

7. *Worship structures are changing.* In the past, most churches operated about the same way, with a call to worship, three hymns, the offering, Bible reading, and a sermon. The challenge—and demand—is for non-traditional formats. Ministers over forty were trained in biblical competence and theological scholarship, but not in storytelling and listening—the demands of immigrants.

My wife, Brenda, spent a week at a retreat center where they taught storytelling. That's what's going on today. Unfortunately, too many seminaries still turn out preachers who read the Bible, exegete the passage, and close with showing how it applies to today's needs.

We're learning that telling and retelling stories—including biblical stories—can be very powerful.

A Bible Story

When we unpack the events and bring out the characters' feelings and tensions, our listeners identify with the story and grasp spiritual truths.

I want to tell the story of Jochebed, the mother of Moses, who decided to float her baby down the river. The story is told in a single verse: "But when she could hide him no longer, she got a papyrus basket for him and coated it with tar and pitch. Then she placed the child in it and put it among the reeds along the bank of the Nile" (Exod. 2:3).

I like to think of this as more than the physical hiding of a baby. It also involved the relationship of a mother and her infant son. Think about the emotional stress of trying to hide a baby every day in a tent while Egyptian soldiers wander through the camp. Whenever they choose to walk through, the mother has to keep the baby quiet, and he can't cry as a normal infant does. This must have caused untold stress for Miriam and Aaron, the older siblings, as well as for the father.

The preservation of that child's life had to be the total focus of Jochebed's life. "But when she could hide him no longer" had to be the day she broke down physically and emotionally. After days and nights of sleepless torment, it had to have been the moment she felt she had failed and cried out, "I can't keep him any longer." She must have walked back and forth, praying, crying, mourning, and trying to figure out what to do.

Then she made her decision by putting him in a waterproof basket and placing the tiny bassinette among the reeds along the banks of the Nile.

All of the anguish and despair is wrapped up in one verse. I find this story so easily imagined. I think of the suffering and hardship, of Jochebed constructing the basket.

"What are you going to do?" I can hear Moses' big sister, Miriam, ask.

"I'm building a little boat."

"What are you going to do with that little boat?"

"I'm going to put your baby brother into it."

The wide-eyed girl asks, "And what's going to happen? There are crocodiles in that river. It's not safe. What happens if—?"

I can imagine Jochebed as she continues to weave that basket and tears flow down her face. Even in those hours of preparation, she remains vigilant. She glances furtively at the little baby.

Finally, she puts him in the basket, and the Bible says, "His sister stood at a distance to see what would happen to him" (v. 4).

When we start telling Bible stories, we don't want to gloss over any like this one simply because it's contained in one verse. We need to pause and consider the toll it takes on the family and what an emotional decision it took to give up the baby. Can we imagine the conversations that went on among the family members? Surely it wasn't an independent decision.

When we unpack stories like that for our listeners, they understand. It's not just the event, but the process that hurts so much.

Once we point to the pain of process, listeners can learn to apply it to their own situations. It is not just coming clean with my husband or my wife, it is not just confessing to my boss what I stole. We see this as the issue of getting from Point A to Point B. Point B is the arrival, but the journey is the story. Once we help people understand about Bible stories and their dynamics, we can show them how all of life is a process. We help them realize what it feels like to give up something we love dearly and the transitions we must go through.

Most people know the rest of the story—that the king's daughter rescued the baby, adopted him as her own, and even hired Jochebed to be Moses' wet nurse. We know the rest of the story, but Jochebed didn't know—and that's what makes storytelling powerful.

Short attention spans are evident in our church pews, so the service has to be done in what I call snippets. That is, worship elements need to be continually changing. Music, drama, and multimedia presentations are interspersed with preaching. Television has conditioned us to expect to receive information in sound bites. That means the church service has to keep moving with no dead moments.

For instance, wise medical people know that. If we visit a savvy doctor, we'll sit in the outside waiting room for a maximum of ten minutes before a receptionist calls our name and ushers us into the inside waiting room. We'll have perhaps another five-minute wait before a nurse comes in and talks to us or takes our blood pressure—some small thing—and then she leaves. This is the pattern. We may have to wait a total of forty-five minutes to an hour, but we have enough happening every few minutes that it doesn't seem as if it's that long.

It also seems as if several people are involved in our case and they keep us moving.

8. *Worship styles are changing.* Worship style will define the congregation. Singing *about* God has shifted to singing *to* God. Many new choruses and praise hymns may not be theologically correct, but they have the style and tempo people want to sing. Futuring churches are trying to incorporate the span of music from pipe organ to rap—all in one service.

The worship team/choir/music department provides a great challenge for any pastor. I've heard some people joke that when the first choir director, Lucifer, fell, he fell right into the choir loft. And there hasn't been any peace since then.

The biggest challenge is for families. Teenagers like one kind of music and their parents like something else, but parents tend to defer to the children because they're willing to do a trade-off. As a parent, I'd rather go to church with my children and have them enjoy it than expect them to put up with music they hate.

People's Baptist Church in Boston, where Dr. Wesley Roberts is pastor, is the oldest African-American church in New England, with huge cathedral ceilings and beautiful crystal glass windows. I was there one Sunday in February—which is Black History Month—to preach at both Sunday morning services.

The service began with pipe organs. Then an immense male chorus sang two spirituals a cappella. Everyone in that group was at least seventy years old, but their voices didn't sound old. One song had to do with traveling on a train, and some of the men sounded like the train and the whistle while the others were singing on the train. It was an emotional time.

After that, they took the offering and made announcements. Then the youth group sang. They sang contemporary music that teens identified with. The service also included traditional singing and well-known hymns as well as a regular choir.

That's an example of a futuring church that can run the gamut from pipe organ to rap all in one service. As I sat on that platform, I smiled and thought, *Here is a church for the whole family. Everybody has an opportunity to get offended, but everyone also has an opportunity to fit in.*

Increasingly, churches will adapt in a number of different ways. It's now common to have different types of services. Friday night could be a contemporary casual format. Early Sunday morning could be traditional and liturgical.

I preached one Sunday at Evangel Church in Chicago. Their first service, which they called the "Get Up Service," was fairly traditional. They called the second one the "Get Down Service." In that service, one choir number lasted a half hour (I timed it), but it had a lot of variation and included congregational participation.

This says that futuring leaders are offering different experiences, and people are attending the services in which the worship style and format fit most of their preferences.

9. Evangelism takes place in both seeker-sensitive as well as more blatant forms. Bill Hybels popularized seeker-sensitive evangelism at Willow Creek, but it's not the only format. Direct, in-your-face evangelism is still being used by growing churches as well.

The most in-your-face evangelism I've seen wasn't done by a loud street evangelist who screamed and pushed tracts into everyone's hands. I was in Brazil in the middle of 2000 at a church with a Sunday night attendance of eight hundred to a thousand people. The pastor said, "All of you who are visiting the church tonight and are already believers, will you please stand?" They did, and he thanked them and told them to be seated. Then he said, "Those of you who are visiting here tonight but are not believers—you have never accepted Jesus Christ as your Savior—will you please stand up?" Maybe a couple dozen people stood.

As I sat there preparing myself to speak, I thought, *I've never seen this before.*

The pastor had already told me, "Sunday night service is get-them-saved night." Consequently, I preached a simple message that Jesus saves. After I finished and the music was playing, I said, "All of you who want to give your life to the Lord, come to the altar." What I didn't realize was that earlier in the service, when these people stood up, they were marked. When I gave the invitation, the "soul winners" who had been assigned to various pews went to those areas. Immediately they were next to those who had stood up. Each carried a Bible, and each spent perhaps ninety seconds explaining salvation before bringing them down to the front. How much more blatant can evangelism get? Yet it worked!

It was totally different from the style I grew up with, where the choir sang fifty stanzas of "Just As I Am" and the pastor intoned, "While every head is bowed and every eye is closed . . .," and then invited the people to come forward, fill out a card, or talk to someone.

We don't need to take sides on how to do evangelism. Various styles work depending on the cultural context. I do know this: Immigrants don't want us to play around. "Tell us what you need or what you want to do. Then I'll tell you whether I'm going to respond." They seem to have no problem saying, "No, I don't think I want to do that right now."

10. *Revival comes in different forms.* Revival itself is being redefined. It used to be the term for a church holding protracted or evangelistic services. Revival now simply means that people who are a part of the community

of believers are empowered to live out the life of Christ in their daily living. One evidence was the WWJD ("What Would Jesus Do?") wristband that was so popular around the year 2000.

The crashing of the planes on September 11, 2001, into the World Trade Center made many people think seriously about God—people who hadn't been inside a church in a decade. Almost all the pastors I spoke with told me that new people came into their churches; others spoke of members making stronger commitments and showing heavier involvement.

Revivals don't always take place inside the church building; they can happen where people live, work, and play as well. They ask, "How can I live out my faith each day?" Immigrants also understand that corporate revival can only happen if individual revival is in place.

When a native prays, "Send us a revival, Lord; send us a revival," he or she is referring to the Lord working in church services. An important evangelist is going to come in and preach, and "People are going to get saved, the church is going to grow and be alive, and we're going to have a great time." After the evangelist leaves, the revival is over.

For the immigrant, revival means, "So now I can learn how to live the faith I have. I'll learn how to transmit my faith to my neighbor."

11. *The church develops rather than trains.* Training is task oriented—a short-term focus on a job that needs to be done. Development focuses more on the person rather than the task, is long term, and is process driven rather than event driven.

Churches that used to do training assumed that if they taught someone how to be an usher, that's all that person did. Those people were good, well-trained ushers. Today these churches develop person-centered abilities and teach people conflict resolution and trouble-shooting skills. In their systemic thinking, they develop them as individuals who have multiple skills, and those same skills can be used in many different places instead of just one defined area.

12. *Education for the church is moving from teaching to learning.* Teaching focuses on the teacher, but learning focuses on the students. When a church looks at its Christian education department, it needs to ask, "What are people learning?" That is, they begin from the end, and their goals drive them.

With approval of the voucher system, home schools will increase along with Christian schools. Future-oriented churches are asking, "How do we hook up with the home school?"

They answer, "Provide a gym, a library, and a music program. Home schoolers need places for social interaction, and their parents need support groups." Future churches are figuring out how to reach out to home schoolers—even those without religious affiliation—and offer assistance with no strings attached. They hook into home school associations in their neighborhood and open church facilities to them, especially the gym. Parents can hold meetings at the church and can establish a good library. The only expense for the church is utilities. Imagine the outreach to the community because home schoolers have a place they can call theirs with no strings attached.

Christian education in futuring churches emphasizes interactive, integrated, and individualized learning. Interactive means there must be a connection between what is being taught and the real world. The stress on individualized instruction demands smaller classrooms, more one-on-one instruction, more parental involvement, and more volunteerism.

The criteria used to be that students studied their Sunday school quarterlies and learned the weekly memory verses. Now the emphasis is "What have you learned that is changing your life? In what ways are you now different because of the lessons?"

The Christian school movement is continuing to grow but in a different way. Previously only large churches had Christian schools; now smaller churches are beginning Christian schools as well. They are more objective or criteria driven, which means teachers will need to know clearly what they are trying to achieve each term or semester. They also need to show how this new knowledge integrates with real life.

No longer is it enough to teach arithmetic just as problems for students to work through. Teachers are now posing real-life issues. "If you go to Kroger with x amount of money and shop . . . " Or "You open a savings account at a local bank and . . . "

Instead of teaching only addition and subtraction, we've seen the need to teach people how to balance their checkbooks. We know two things about Americans and their checking accounts. First, most Americans accept the figures on their bank statements without verifying them. Second, many of them don't know how to reconcile their bank statements with their checkbooks. Teaching people how to balance their checkbooks is important, because, as stewardship institutes have taught us, people who regularly balance their checkbooks are better givers.

I visited one large academy for grades pre-K through six. Every classroom has three computers, and they have an Internet-active computer lab. Charles Schwab, the investing company, has partnered with the school and set up every classroom with a business that seeded the class a small amount of money, about one hundred dollars. Each class has had to devise a business plan and sell a product. Money earned is divided among the stockholders of the company—the students. If they want to spin off another company, the stockholders can decide not to take the money but to invest it. That's integrated learning in the real world.

I also see in the future smaller, more individualized classrooms with higher levels of parent involvement and more volunteerism.

13. *Leadership teams replace single leaders.* "None of us is as good as all of us." In the past, one person led everything, but immigrants want to be part of the leadership team.

As I've mentioned elsewhere, there was a time when the pastor stood behind the pulpit and said, "Thus saith the Lord," and most of the church members went along without question. Today's immigrants want to be part of a winning team. Therefore, they are willing to take orders from a coach and change their style of playing to win the game. They are not, however, willing to submit to autocratic control. That means that in futuring churches, dialogue comes before decision. The process is more important than the destination.

14. *Decisions are made by consensus.* Futuring churches hand down fewer executive decisions and try to operate by consensus instead. Leaders aren't trying to get people to announce whether they're for or against anything. Rather, they work until there is general agreement. They're trying to get everyone to see the larger picture. Once that happens, wisdom emerges for the greater good.

15. *Church governments are changing.* Church boards and committees are being replaced by teams, and within the teams are subgroups or task forces: Task forces have the ability to make faster short- and long-term decisions, because they have one task to do and that's the end of their responsibility. Churches that are going to reach and hold the dot.com crowd can't wait two years to make a decision. They're risk takers, and they want change

now. The essence of their thinking is that if they wait one more day, they are that much farther behind.

16. *The church is being forced to rethink sexuality.* The three major issues are women in ministry, homosexuality, and abortion. Other issues include cohabitation outside of marriage and women choosing to have a family without having relations with a man. Churches need to define their stand on such issues, and the best time to do so is when they are not involved with one of these problems. The best time to talk about something is when there's nothing to talk about. No church is going to be exempt from all of these issues, no matter how biblical the church might view itself to be.

17. *The demand for excellence increases.* In preaching, the demand for excellence isn't on the knowledge of biblical languages and polished illustrations. Immigrants seek authenticity and integrity. In teaching, they demand substance and not the lightweight material we have used in recent years. The third demand is for relevance—preaching with the Bible in one hand and the newspaper in the other.

Although my friend Allen Skelton was a successful pastor, he had to file for personal bankruptcy. In the midst of that ordeal he preached one of the most memorable sermons I've ever heard. He told us the mistakes he had made and was totally vulnerable. He explained how he paid off American Express with Visa and Visa with MasterCard and MasterCard with Discover. He talked about the whole thing: about spending and income and mismanagement and lack of planning. In the midst of all that, he connected with us.

One of the reasons T. D. Jakes is a phenomenal communicator is that he goes to the point of need and relates back to when he was in need. He identifies with people and gives them points of connection. That's what immigrants want.

18. *Church leaders are being held to stricter require-ments.* It's still relatively easy to join a congregation, but those who aspire to leadership will face heavier demands. The church I attend has a weekly attendance of 180 to 190 every Sunday. Even though small, we have leadership development meetings for everyone in any type of leadership. It's done in phases, and those who haven't completed phase one may not go on to phase two. No one can serve in leadership before completing phase two. Five years ago, going through such a pro-gram was voluntary; it is now required.

New Birth Missionary Baptist Church in Lithonia, Georgia, has a membership of twenty-six thousand. Before anyone can take on a leadership role in that church, they must have completed thirty-three hours of a Minister in Training course at Beulah Heights.

A supervisor may call us at any time and say, "Wanda Jones has applied for _____ position. Where is she on the program?"

"Out of thirty-three hours, she has completed seven-teen."

The supervisor will then make a decision about whether that's enough credits to apply for the position. The supervisor may say to Wanda, "You need to com-plete at least eight more hours before we'll consider you for this leadership role."

I've also observed that many futuring churches make covenants built around what I call the "what-ifs." Such a covenant will spell out requirements for being a leader and consequences for failing to meet those require-ments. For example, if a leader fails to tithe, such and such will happen.

When immigrants are being serviced, they want to know that those who serve them are competent. They know that competency means continuous learning. Why, for example, would a church let me teach Sunday school if I had never been through all the necessary training? If I'm in computers, I have to keep going to school all the time. If I'm a dentist or a heart surgeon, I have to keep up with new technology. So in the mind of immigrants, it makes sense for leaders to be on the cutting edge.

Because many immigrants are unwilling to join (they don't want to obligate themselves), some churches are willing to use nonmembers—as long as they have been through the required training process.

19. *Immigrants seek a vision- and purpose-driven church.* They ask church leaders, "What is your purpose? Why are you here?" They want to devote their time, energy, and resources to worthwhile projects. When immigrants consider giving to the Lord, the local church isn't usually their first thought, which runs contrary to the thinking of natives. Immigrants take their resources to where they see people of vision and purpose wisely using them.

20. *Discipline in the church is expected and implemented.* In the working world, there are consequences for failing to do quality work. The church also expects competence. Formerly in the church, *discipline* was a bad word, but that's changing. Churches generally have a set of guidelines for leaders. If they don't meet those standards of competence, they do not stay in leadership. Sunday school teachers, for example, are required to attend quarterly teacher training classes. If they don't, they are removed. The word then gets out that the church has high standards. They want their teachers to be well qualified for what they are doing. And they want parents to feel that they can entrust their children to those teachers.

Consider this: If I was a public school student and did not show up for football practice, I would not be able to play in the next game. In the church, though, if I miss choir practice, I can still robe up and walk into the choir loft.

But that's changing. The choir director may say, "Sam, if you don't practice with us, you can't sing with us."

21. *Relevancy is in demand.* Immigrants ask, "Why?" Church leaders can no longer say, "Everyone knows that. . . . " We have to explain things to immigrants, because they may question what natives took for granted. And native leaders need to understand that immigrants' questions aren't signs of disagreement; they simply show their need for clarification.

"I'm not questioning authority," an immigrant says, "but why do I have to attend three out of four meetings? I'm already a public school teacher with ten years of experience. I also have a Bible college diploma. So why do I have to come?"

If native leaders get offended, they've missed the point. A response that will make sense to immigrants is: "We have requirements that every person—without exception—must meet so that *we* know they're qualified. We want no one to slip in just because of their background."

22. *Immigrants stress effectiveness and measurable benchmarks.* Natives may state their goals as "We want to reach our world for Jesus." Immigrants are more specific. They say, "We will try to reach people within a one-mile radius of our church. Our goal is to see one hundred people receive the Lord as their Savior. We want to see thirty-five people go through our discipleship program." They have definite benchmarks so that at the end of the year or planning cycle they can check their progress. Either they made their goals or they didn't.

They won't be able to say, as natives have in the past, "We haven't gained any, but we haven't lost any either. We're still holding the fort; we're faithful. God is blessing our faithfulness." If the native church loses members, their ready answer is, "God is purifying and culling us. He's getting us ready for something new." Those aren't satisfactory responses to immigrants.

23. *Family time is a premium consideration.* Natives stopped work on Friday and had the weekend to themselves. This is no longer true, and immigrants are tied up on Saturday with a variety of activities. They seek ways to get their spirituality—but not at the expense of further dividing family time. Native leaders bragged about the activity level at the church. Immigrants are asking, "How can we coordinate all these activities?"

In native thinking, a church was successful if the pastor could brag, "We have something going on all the time. On Monday night we have men's Bible study, Tuesday night we have women's Bible study, Wednesday night we have family Bible study, Thursday we have youth group, Friday we have evangelism," and their list went on.

No more. Family needs are now making parents ask, "How can we coordinate things? If we want to go to midweek activities, can we all go Friday night? The kids can go to their place, my wife can go to the ladies' place, I can go to the men's place, and then we can get back together for twenty minutes of celebration and be on our way."

> In November 2001 the U.S. Census Bureau estimated that the percentage of married metro-Atlanta residents has fallen from 57 to 54 percent since the 1990 census. Similar patterns and figures are true for other large cities.

24. *Pastoral care has higher demands.* The needs of dysfunctional people and families will cause congregations to "out-source" pastoral care. They will have to bring in chaplains who do nothing but hospital care or counseling. Churches may choose to do out-sourcing not necessarily with someone who has no connection with the church, but with someone from whom they can cut away and say, "That is them; this is us."

25. *Future churches recognize and respond to single-parent homes.* At least ten million single mothers live in America. Churches need to minister to them as well as to those who have never married and those who are widowed or divorced. Churches are rethinking traditional couples' dinners and Valentine's dates. What used to be the fifth wheel will become the majority in some churches.

The New American Family

- If you don't have a child at home, you're in the majority. Today only 34 percent of U.S. households have children under the roof.
- Fewer couples are getting married.
- More than 50 percent of those who marry for the first time were previously living together.
- Single motherhood is a growing option. Unmarried mothers now account for 33 percent of all births in the United States.
- The changing patterns of the new American family will influence decisions on parental leave, day care, and other major social issues.*

*Rutgers University National Merit Project

26. *The number of younger retirees continues to grow.* People are retiring at an earlier age, and they have extra time and talent for involvement, not just in the church, but also in the community.

27. *America is getting grayer.* If the American Association of Retired Persons became a nation, it would be the thirtieth largest nation in the world, slightly smaller in population than Argentina.

- By 2025 more than 35 percent of Americans will be over age 50. (Currently the figure is 27 percent.)
- By 2020 more than 105 million people in the United States will be over age 55.

- These figures will involve all of us in issues of health care and pastoral care.
- By 2025, for the first time in history, seven generations will live side by side. The church will have to struggle with different worship forms and styles to meet those different generations.
- Assisted living care hit the $86 billion mark in 1986. It is expected to grow to $490 billion in 2030.
- Roughly 23 percent of Americans are over 50, and one in five is over 65.
- 13 million Americans care for their parents in their homes.
- When we include those who are caregivers of parents but don't live with them, the number doubles.
- Most seniors live below the poverty line.
- The average life expectancy of Americans is 76 years.
- In 2001, 54.7 percent of people age 65 and older lived with their spouses, 12.8 percent lived with other relatives, and only 2.2 percent lived with nonrelatives.
- The 30.3 percent who lived alone were in communities with other seniors.

The National Hospice Foundation found that half of Americans want their families to carry out their final wishes, but 75 percent haven't explained what their wishes are. Seventy thousand Americans are one hundred years old or older.

The churches in the North are losing older members, so what do you do without them? They are the ones who kept the doors open. On the other hand, the influx of people in Florida and Arizona and places in the Sunbelt makes church leaders there ask, "What do we do with them?"

Churches are struggling with how to tap into the volunteer base among the elderly who are financially stable. Many of them are healthy, and they have accumulated wisdom and have more free time than any other group. Most of all, seniors want to make the last years count.

> In times of change, it is the learners who will inherit the earth, while the learned will find themselves beautifully equipped for a world that no longer exists.
>
> Author unknown

I know of at least ten growing churches that are building senior citizen apartments right on the church complexes. Those leaders see the future and are preparing for it now—right on the church property.

28. *We have the mall motif—everything under one roof.* Fast-growing mega-churches have their own bookstores, gyms, weight rooms, cafeterias, and childcare facilities. This means that futuring churches are becoming more entrepreneurial. The bookstore may be run by someone outside the church. The church is following the mall concept. The big anchor stores such as Sears and J. C. Penney don't own their buildings; they lease them from the mall developer. This is increasingly the mind-set of growing churches.

I've been in churches that have so many international members that they sell products from the countries represented—headgear, handbags, shirts, dresses, and novelty items. Why not sell them? The church benefits, and individuals do too.

29. *Multimedia will be an increasing reality.* Because immigrants are visual learners, future church leaders increasingly use visual forms of communication. At our church when the pastor preaches, his main points are scrolling on a screen right above him.

30. *Technology—e-mail, connecting people—will have major implications for how we do ministry, especially*

in global missions. Mail used to take weeks to get to other countries, but with e-mail we can communicate in real time and take immediate actions. Services such as UPS, FedEx, and DHL have speeded up the world. They specialize in overseas mail and guarantee that any size package will reach its destination within three days.

31. *Consumerism has come to church.* Future-oriented churches are providing leadership, education, diet, exercise, and a lot of other things. People can buy Christian exercise videos, books or tapes of Christian business principles, and self-help books. Congregations will learn to do packaging to reach out to consumers and to resource them. For instance, the pastor of a growing church will have tapes and books and resources available for the people.

32. *Money is now plentiful.* There's an unprecedented transfer of wealth. The bottom line is this: Trillions of dollars are going to be flowing from one generation down to the next, and that generation is fairly well set themselves. The giving generation is now saying, "I want to leave my estate in a legacy that will be worthwhile rather than fund somebody's lifestyle."

Philanthropy has taken on huge roles. How success is measured has changed. A growing number of Christian philanthropists measure success by the amount of money given away.

Don Chapman is one example. Don can't help but start new businesses, and he's a multimillionaire. He sold his

> The number of tax-exempt charitable, religious, educational, scientific, and literary organizations in the United States grew by 74 percent between 1991 and 2001.
>
> *Atlanta Journal-Constitution,* July 21, 2001, quoting an Independent Sector report

company, S & S Tug—the company that builds tractors that push planes out of their gates—on Friday, and on Monday he started a new company called Legacy Ventures. His new company raises venture capital, and his immediate goal was to raise $150 million for venture capital in two months.

He said to me one morning over breakfast, "You know, I'm at a place in my life where I really don't have to do all of this. I want to give my life to something. I haven't discovered just what it is." He was still searching, but he knew one important thing—philanthropy isn't just writing a check—it's becoming part of the action.

33. *Financial accountability is a must.* Immigrants are not interested in micromanaging, but they want to see the larger picture. Future churches regularly publish one-page financial statements or broad categories of income and expenses that provide the information immigrants want to know.

34. *Urbanization or cross-cultural shifts are becoming the rule.* By the year 2025, more than 38 percent of Americans will be ethnic minorities, and Hispanics will be the largest minority. Urbanization means that the trend of moving to the suburbs will shift as people move back into the cities. This movement will throw people into a cross-cultural world, so church leaders need to understand the variety of cultures that will become the mainstay of churches and businesses.

35. *The concept of missions is changing.* No longer is the church thinking of missions only as work in foreign lands; now they're including urban areas and inner cities. International missionaries are focusing on the United States.

Furthermore, the church is moving toward short-term rather than long-term missions. In the old days, missionaries served four years with a fifth year of furlough. For example, in 1995 BHBC began Missions Overseas

Short Term (M.O.S.T.). Since then up to eighty people have received cross-cultural training and gone to another country to serve. They receive college credit because it's part of their core curriculum.

Another change is that instead of being *sending* agencies, churches are becoming *going* agencies. More and more churches are going churches rather than sending churches. For example, Atlanta's Mount Paran Church of God, under Dr. David Cooper's leadership, has missionaries in thirty-eight countries. Almost all of them are former members of Mount Paran. I spoke at their missions conference, and during that one week, they raised $1.5 million. That means that people within a local church are raising substantial support for missionaries, which fosters the idea, "We are part of this. We are going with them."

Even if missionaries stay in a foreign country for a year, they're not out of contact with the home church. When they return, they don't have to spend a year doing what we used to refer to as deputation work, raising funds to return. Those with denominational support haven't always had that pressure, of course. Even so, the trend is still to raise total support for a family or individual within the congregation.

Inner-city missions is an area Beulah Heights Bible College is emphasizing and training people for. We used to spend a lot of money going across the ocean yet did little here at home. Now we're refocusing and seeing how much we need to do right here in the United States. We're growing new churches—often sponsored by larger congregations—and we're calling that missions.

36. *Social action is receiving a strong emphasis—especially partnership with government programs.* Because of collaborative government funding, there is an explosion of nonprofit organizations. The federal government won't give money to a church, but they will give to other

types of nonprofit groups, so some churches are incorporating as nonprofit under a different name with a separate board. Corporations are also more open to funding such nonprofit groups.

Social action is done in partnership with government programs. The 501(c)3 nonprofit organizations are exploding around us because there is more collaborative government money available through the Department of Housing and Urban Development (HUD), the Department of Education, and especially through the rehab sections of our city governments. The issue of separation of church and state doesn't even come into play when HUD gives money to a nonprofit group because they're serving the homeless. It's the same ministry your church would have been doing, but now the government is funding it.

37. *Futuring churches are increasingly active in local politics.* Churches can't endorse candidates; however, people from within the church are being encouraged to run for school boards and county commissions with the unofficial support of their church.

For example, in early 2000, Hooters, a restaurant with scantily clad waitresses, wanted to open a franchise in Fayetteville, Georgia, but the community packed the hearing room for the zoning and defeated the petition. They also let politicians know that they were facing an increasingly vocal constituency.

Christians involved in politics hold their meetings off church property. Increasingly, futuring congregations are saying, "We will not take a backseat and leave the driving up to others. We will help put our own people in the driver's seat."

For immigrants, *politics* has been redefined as a process through which community values are implemented. *Politics* used to be a bad word. Pastors would say, "We don't have politics in our church." What they didn't recognize is that we have politics in our churches, our homes, and our workplaces—wherever people are involved. Immigrants are saying, "Because this is the case, let's see how this works, get into the process, and make a positive contribution."

38. *Church and state issues change.* In 1998 former Senator John Ashcroft sponsored a bill called Charitable Choice that gave corporations permission to donate money to faith-based institutions and receive tax deductions on those gifts. The White House, under the direction of George W. Bush, set up a division called Faith-Based Community Initiatives. Now future-facing churches can compete for and receive money for faith-based childcare centers, rehab centers, hospice centers, subsidized housing, and other projects.

39. *Shared church facilities will increase.* More churches are constructing multipurpose buildings in which they set up chairs on Sunday for worship and play volleyball and basketball on Monday and Wednesday. Other churches with traditional buildings are sharing the facilities with Christian groups. I foresee that two or more congregations will jointly own facilities.

Churches are also building auditoriums separate from the church and renting the space for such things as banquets and weddings. As long as they report it as unrelated income, the IRS allows it.

40. *The doctrine of tolerance remains an immense challenge to the health of the church.* Christians want to be inclusive and not hurt others, but unless we're especially cautious, the lines will continue to blur and the Christian edges will become soft.

I see this as the greatest challenge to the health of the church. How do we become so inclusive that we don't hurt anyone and yet draw the line on behavior and practices that are contrary to our beliefs? For instance, how do we continue to stress the love of God for everyone, accept Muslims and Hindus as people loved by God, and yet draw the line?

Some churches have become so tolerant that they are saying, in effect, it doesn't matter what people believe. This is the great danger we face, because we're then apt to believe anything. As Christians, at some point we have to say, "This is what we believe. This is the core of our faith. You don't have to believe as we do, but don't try to make us embrace your faith."

In 1998 I faced the issue of exclusivity. I had arranged a meeting for twenty influential Christian leaders in the area. We met in our college atrium around a table of refreshments. Within five minutes after our meeting began, one of the leaders sat down across from me and stared right at me. He represented an organization that stresses inclusivity and especially embraces the homosexual community. "Dr. Chand, what would be your feelings toward diversity and inclusivity?" he asked.

I knew where he was going with it, but I said, "I think you'll have to further define that a little bit for me."

"All right. To whom would you not give a cup of cold water?"

"Nobody comes to my mind. We'll give a cup of cold water to anybody."

"So tell me then, who all can sit around this table?"

All the others sitting at the table had stopped talking and were listening intently. "Let me just cut to the chase. We will give a cup of cold water to homosexuals, bisexuals, transsexuals—that does not matter to us. We will serve any- and everybody without prejudice. *However,* the core group—the team—that facilitates this process will not be those of that persuasion."

"You mean to tell me that lesbians and gays will not be welcome to be part of the decision-making process?"

"That is exactly what I'm saying to you."

"Well, I don't think we can work together." He picked up his folder and stood up.

"I appreciate your time," I said. "You have been thoughtful to come today."

I did nothing to hold him back or placate him. And no one else at the table said anything to encourage him to stay. I must admit that as he walked away I was thinking, *There goes the support of almost two thousand churches.*

As much as I hated to see that pastor leave, I also knew that tolerance could go only so far. It must have a stopping point—and it does with all of us, perhaps at different places. If we have no unbreachable line, we will soon become corrupt at our core and become so soft that we lose our identity.

That is exactly what happened with God's people in the Old Testament. After they moved into the Promised Land, they slowly absorbed the culture and religious beliefs of their neighbors. In time, "everyone did as he saw fit" (Judg. 21:25).

41. *The church is suffering and will suffer persecution.* More people were martyred in the twentieth century than in the rest of the centuries combined, especially in countries such as the Sudan, China, Pakistan, and India. The church has always thrived under persecution, and that's when purification takes place.

Persecution in the United States will be more subtle. Groups such as the American Civil Liberties Union blatantly oppose the church, but we will see more subtle forms in the workplace and with individuals, especially because we believe Jesus provides the only way to God. An accusation of intolerance may well be the most powerful weapon raised against Christians.

42. *Cult activity and satanic powers continue to have a great influence on our world.* Multiculturalism also brings pluralism, and that opens the doors to every religion.

> Futuring leaders are flexi-
> ble and are already con-
> sidering ways to respond
> to new challenges.

Twenty years ago, who would have believed that a city in the Deep South would have Hindu temples and Muslim mosques?

Other gods are coming to America via people from a higher economic level than the average factory worker. More than half of the 35,000 East Indians who live in Atlanta are professionals who have power, organization, and money.

The church has two ways to approach this situation. The first is to become an apologetic congregation—in the true sense of the word. That doesn't mean we need to apologize for our stance, but that we know what we believe and defend or speak up for it. The second approach is to educate Christians to know the reality of the faith, to teach them so that they are fully grounded in the faith. They may not know how to answer every argument raised by Muslims, but they can become so familiar with the real that the counterfeit will not feel right. When the kind and highly educated neighbor who lives in a beautiful house and drives a Mercedes Benz tries to introduce them to a new way of thinking, they will be able to discern that it is wrong.

Perhaps an illustration will help. In the old days, when banks trained tellers to deal with cash, one of the final areas of their training was the vault. For hours they did nothing but feel money. The idea was that their fingers would become so sensitive that they would know a counterfeit when they touched it.

Likewise, futuring churches have to train their members to detect counterfeit religions. We have to be more biblically-based in teaching the fundamentals of the truth so that our members can easily detect the counterfeit.

43. *Both false prophets and true prophets are emerging.* Anybody who has money can buy airtime, so we'll see

a mixture of false and true prophets on TV. Web sites also are leading people down strange paths.

Cec Murphey went to the Internet to look up *Light and Life* magazine, put out by the Free Methodist Church, after one of their editors asked him to write an article. He discovered that a New Age group had bought that domain name.

The worst false prophets will be those who are close to the truth and say enough of the right words so that they are seductive and lead many astray.

44. *Future churches live and flourish with contradictions.* Traditions of the past are now being pushed aside, and there is no longer just one right way to do things. This touches everything from music to social activities. Living with contradictions will increasingly become a part of who we are and what we do. Futuring leaders and their congregations are willing to embrace contradictions and live at peace.

I present these forty-four trends as catalysts to challenge future thinking.

My biggest concern is that natives continue to broadcast on AM and immigrants have tuned in to FM. Nothing is wrong with either of their receivers. But no matter how good the receiver, we don't get both frequencies at the same time. The AM stations are crying out, "If only people were more committed," while the FM stations are saying, "How will this bring meaning to me?"

In this chapter I've tried to point out the issues that futuring leaders and all Christian congregations are facing or will face in the near future. Now let's look at the kind of leadership we need to go boldly into that looming future.

FIFTEEN

Five Major Appeals

Just because we may be motivated does not mean others will sense or feel the same inspiration. In fact, I constantly hear wailing statements such as:

"If only people were more committed."

"If only they would rise to the challenge."

Earlier I said that duty is dead in the church. So what do we do after the death of duty? What do we do when obligation is unemployed? Duty-motivated natives took responsibilities and stayed with those commitments. Yet some Sunday school teachers, for instance, should have quit years before they did. Why did they stay on? It's obvious: They continued out of a sense of duty and loyalty. "I made a commitment, and I can't let them down. What will they do without me?"

Duty as a motivating fuel has lost its effectiveness. Therefore, I want to suggest that there are five motivational fuels for the flourishing twenty-first-century church and then conclude with the ones that are the most effective. First we need to pause and ask: Which of these appeals would energize God's people in this century? What frequency are we broadcasting on? What frequency are the people in our church tuned in to?

1. *Compassion.* Compassion is other-centered. It describes sharing with one another, serving and caring for others, giving to others, and behaving lovingly toward others.
2. *Community.* This is where we have our roots, our place of belonging. Even in our fragmented world, people want to belong more now than ever before. People find community in country clubs, hunting clubs, churches, and volunteer and civic organizations, because all of us want and need to belong. Community also includes relationships with family and friends.
3. *Challenge.* We urge others to attain more, to accomplish more, and to achieve more with their lives.
4. *Reasonability.* We appeal to data, logic, analysis, and good sense.
5. *Commitment.* We appeal to loyalty, duty, obligation, or vows.

Of these five motivational fuels leaders use, I believe that churches that stress compassion and community will thrive the best in the coming years. Why not the others? Let's examine them.

- *Challenge.* When people come to our church, we fail to realize that they've been challenged all week long to obtain more, accomplish more, and achieve more. They don't want to be pushed, and they are seeking something different. If they go to a church where challenge is the motivating fuel, that's just like another day of the week for them.

- *Reasonability.* Although reasonability sounds good, again that's what people are involved with all day long, every day of the work week. They're overwhelmed with data, logic, analysis, and good sense whether they're salespeople, CEOs, or schoolteachers. When they come to a place of worship, why would they want the same appeal?

- *Commitment.* We make a serious mistake when we plead for commitment too soon. We know that just because they sign a pledge card doesn't mean they're committed. Commitment is an issue of the heart, and, therefore, appealing to commitment scares people away rather than invites them in.

> People used to come to church on Sundays to *celebrate* the community they lived with all week. Now they come to church on Sunday or Friday or Saturday to *find* the community they don't have the rest of the week.

This leaves us with two inviting, motivating fuels: compassion and community.

Compassion refers to connecting at a "soul level," and our motivation is beyond reciprocity and self-indulgence. It is other-focused. At the end of our lives, we then recognize meaningful fulfillment at a deeper level than if we had just done many good deeds.

Compassion involves five qualities: sharing, caring, giving, loving, and serving.

Community is about connections with an emphasis on commonality. Our individualistic society has driven us back to the beginnings of God's plan for the human race. We were created as gregarious community dwellers. Our deepest need is to be with others and to weave a common bond. Our penal system, for example, shows this clearly. Aside from execution, the harshest punishment is for a prisoner to be placed in solitary confinement.

People today want to feel that they are a vital part of a group; that is, they want to experience community. For at least a century we've pushed for individuality. Now we're realizing that that has led to a hunger to be part of a group or organization.

> **Appeal to duty has lost its effectiveness, but futuring leaders can appeal to compassion, community, challenge, reasonability, and commitment.**

A few years ago, the top-rated TV sitcom was *Cheers*. The theme song of that show said that people hung out at that community bar because everyone knew their name. The bar represented the communal relationship for the characters who passed through every week.

In corporations, almost everyone works in cubicles. So where do they meet for community? Many businesses have an unofficial hangout where employees go after work to wind down before they go home and to reconnect with human beings after sitting in front of machines all day.

Although we live in an individualistic society, our need to connect strongly pulls us into community. The church has a great opportunity to reach out and meet that need.

SIXTEEN

Living in EPIC Times

We live in EPIC times. This is an acrostic.

Experiential says, "We've talked enough. Stop talking and just do it."

Participatory says, "Count me in. I want to participate in this."

Icon-driven says, "You have to draw the picture for me. Let me see it for myself."

Connection says, "That connects with me. I want to belong."

The best way I can illustrate that is to point to the amazing success of eBay, Inc., *without advertising*. This company describes itself as one that "provides person-to-person trading community on the Internet where buyers and sellers are brought together." eBay is worth more than many of the anchor chain stores at our malls. They are successful because they understand the times.

Those of us trained in the last century were trained with words. We put emphasis on what we said and how we said it. Today people learn with pictures. Preachers and teachers who paint with words are master communicators. We can take listeners where we want them to go if they can "see" what we mean.

My cowriter says he tells new writers, "Close your eyes when you're not sure about a word. Can you see the word?" He gives them a series of words. If he says "trees" that's not visual, because it's vague and general. If he says, "oak" or "blue cedar," he has given them a picture. Is it any wonder that Windows is built on icons?

In the final chapter I point out the five challenges futuring leaders in all areas of the church face.

SEVENTEEN

New Leadership Styles

Like all faithful Jews, Joseph and Mary took their twelve-year-old son, Jesus, to the Passover feast in Jerusalem (see Luke 2:41–52). This wasn't their first trip; in fact, it was a trip they took every year to follow the Old Testament law. Thus, it was a tradition—the way they did things. Tradition isn't bad, but for some people, repetitiveness finally loses its meaning.

I'm going to spiritualize this story—that is, I'm going to speak of events and people as symbolic. I'm quite aware that was not Luke's intent in writing the story; but by spiritualizing it, I can use it to show the native versus immigrant mentality more clearly.

Joseph and Mary represent the old church, or the natives. Jesus represents the immigrants, or the new church. In this well-known story, after the feast, Jesus' parents leave and assume Jesus is with them. While his parents start their return to Nazareth to live as usual, Jesus stays in Jerusalem. He's there beginning to fulfill his calling.

If you are or seek to become a futuring leader, here are five challenges you need to face:

1. Focus the majority of your efforts on the future.
2. Understand the fundamental nature of change.
3. Appreciate complex systems and how they work.
4. Examine your leadership style.
5. Create a shared vision to build bridges to the future.

For three days, Mary and Joseph do not even know that Jesus is not with them, which is a way of saying that many of our churches don't even know that they've stopped being effective. They're still doing what they were doing; for them, it's business as usual. They may have started out exciting and innovative, but they don't realize that they have lost the cutting edge.

What happens when Mary and Joseph discover the boy is gone? They do the obvious—they search for him among the familiar, among relatives and friends, but Jesus isn't there.

They do some serious thinking and return to the place where they last saw their son. This is like going back to where the church lost its cutting edge. They finally find him and are shocked at their discovery.

Four things are going on in verses 46 and 47:

1. Jesus *listens* to the traditional leaders—the priests and teachers.
2. Jesus *asks* questions.
3. Jesus *understands* their answers.
4. Jesus *gives* them answers.

Notice that Jesus did three things before he gave answers. That's characteristic of effective futuring leaders.

First, if you are going to be such a leader, you need to listen. Listen to what people—especially the people in your congregation—are saying.

Second, after you've heard, ask questions for clarification. Stay at it until you've asked all the relevant questions.

Third, ponder their responses and understand the issues and needs. Don't be in a hurry to solve issues or give great advice. Don't do anything until you're sure you understand the complexity of the situation.

Finally, you're prepared to give answers—but only after you have gone through the first three steps.

Jesus' parents return to the place where they left their son. They retrace their steps. As soon as Mary sees Jesus, she asks, "Why are you treating us this way?" She's asking the "us versus them" question. Why are *you* treating *us* this way?

This is the point of tension between the natives and the immigrants. Jesus doesn't really answer, but he points out that he must be about the Father's business.

In the traditional church, there is tension between the business of the church and the business of the kingdom. The immigrant is more kingdom oriented while the natives are still locked into the traditions of the past.

Mary and Joseph merely shook their heads. They didn't get it. How could this kid know so much and be so bright? They were older and had been part of the Jewish system all their lives, yet he was showing them up. That's a way to say that if futuring leaders expect the natives to understand immigrant thinking, they can forget it. Too often it is impossible for natives to make that mental adjustment. Futuring leaders have learned to live with this tension between the two groups. It's also true that most of the time the immigrants won't understand the natives.

The hopeful note in this story is the way it ends. "Then [Jesus] returned to Nazareth with them and was obedient to them; and his mother stored all these things in her heart" (Luke 2:51 NLT). An older translation says that she "pondered these things."

Mary, the native, didn't just ignore or deny what she heard. Later, when Jesus had completed his ministry and died on the cross, his mother was there. Somehow the native had learned to think like an immigrant.

Finally, I want to conclude by giving church leaders five suggestions for becoming more effective futurefaith leaders.

1. *Focus the majority of your efforts on the future.* Even though I exhort leaders to think of the future, I'm aware that most of their followers are bogged down in the present. They're coping with getting their children to soccer practice on time, paying off their credit card balances, recovering from divorce, or worrying about putting a parent in a nursing facility. Effective leaders acknowledge this and try to be available to help in any way possible. While they wrap arms around the dazed or hurting, they also keep a large portion of their attention fixed on the future. They need to see the crises that are still too far ahead for problem-plagued members to grapple with.

> Growing churches don't hire a pastor to do youth ministry. That puts a lid on the youth. Instead, they hire a youth pastor to train other youth leaders—and they remove the lid.

They need to foresee the problems—and opportunities—that will face the congregation in a few weeks or months. If they are properly focused, drastic changes won't take them by surprise, *and* they'll have their people prepared to cope with them.

2. *Understand the fundamental nature of change.* New paradigms show up before we need them, and they take the unprepared by surprise. Stay in touch with the out-

side world, and don't allow yourself to be confined to your congregation or your denomination. Most of the time, those who are not part of the present system introduce changes. Too many insiders accept life as it is and often push away anything that demands change.

Suppose, for example, your niche is Christian education and you know you need to make major changes in order to be fully effective. Consider bringing in someone who is not part of your church but is a Christian education specialist. Such people can bring about the greatest changes in your organization.

At Beulah Heights, we brought in a new comptroller, Maxine Marks, whom we hired from St. Elizabeth's College in New Jersey. Once Maxine joined our staff, she brought about fresh perspective. "Why do you do that? Have you considered . . . ?" She questioned our procedures and attitudes and taught us new and better methods of accounting.

One warning, of course, is that a team has to be secure to accept an outsider coming in and making changes. If team members are secure and committed to doing their best, they can work through all of that and even celebrate the challenge.

You, as the leader, need to understand the fundamental nature of change. Ask yourself, "What is change, and how do I bring about change?" If you're a futuring leader, you'll make change a major part of your study. You have to become a specialist in the area of change or your leadership just won't be effective in this century.

3. *Appreciate complex systems and how they work.* How does your church fit into the community? How does the community fit into your city? How does the city fit into the county? How does all of that come back to your church? How do the people in your church interweave their lives with you and your staff? When a family goes through troubled times, how does that bear on the way

your church functions? Once we understand complex systems and how they interrelate, we can become effectively involved in the systems and in change.

4. *Examine your leadership style.* Too few church leaders pause to think carefully about their leadership style. Often they assume there is only one way to lead and don't question whether they might learn a better style.

I suggest you start with several questions:

- What is my delegation style?
- Do I dump or do I delegate?
- Do I give authority and then yank it back?
- Do I need to be in control of every situation?

You are a leader, and I have never met a strong leader who didn't have some problems with control. That's probably one reason you are a leader! The downside is it goes back to the lid or the ceiling of the helium-filled balloon. That's the ceiling on your productivity.

Here are more self-study questions:

- Do you manage your time well?
- Are you organized or haphazard?
- Do you start each day with a sense of what you need to accomplish next?

5. *Create a shared vision to build bridges to the future.* The emphasis here is on shared vision. In the church, people need your vision, but they also want a voice in their future. Effective futuring leaders build bridges and encourage others to join them on the journey across the bridge. Shared visions mean, "It isn't my vision; it's our vision."

Leaders Who Develop Leaders

I'm immensely indebted to Dr. John Maxwell, who helps us understand the difference between leaders who develop followers and leaders who develop leaders in the following material.

Futurefaith leaders in growing churches know:

- To *add* growth, leaders gather and train followers; to *multiply* growth, they gather and train other leaders.
- 90 percent of all leaders gather followers and not leaders.
- Leaders are hard to find, hard to gather, and hard to hold.
- Leaders who develop followers *need* to be needed; leaders who develop leaders *want* to be needed.
- Leaders who develop followers focus on people's *weaknesses;* leaders who develop leaders focus on people's *strengths.*
- Leaders who develop followers devote their attention to the bottom 20 percent; leaders who develop leaders devote their attention to the top 20 percent.
- Leaders who develop followers lift up themselves; leaders who develop leaders lift up others.
- Leaders who develop followers *spend* time with people; leaders who develop leaders *invest* time with people.
- Leaders who develop followers ask for little commitment; leaders who develop leaders ask for much commitment.
- Leaders who develop followers lead everyone the same way; leaders who develop leaders lead everyone differently.
- Leaders who develop followers impact the present generation; leaders who develop leaders impact the next generation.

Conclusion

Someone once said, "Everything we see today came about because someone first thought about it." That's obvious, but many of us tend to forget what goes on before the action. Thinking, conceptualizing, and planning must

> Futuring leaders focus on the future even though they know their followers are concerned with the present.

come first. I've observed many leaders who become highly excited over activity (visible) but have little regard for transformational thinking (invisible). They quickly engage in "making things happen" instead of standing back and considering the process and the effects of their action in the months and years ahead.

One primary purpose of this book is to underscore the need for atypical ways of thinking that lead to different conclusions and thus envision new strategies. Thus, futuring calls us to contextualize leadership and view it as a process rather than a set of activities.

As we move into tomorrow with our leadership, here are two things we need to keep before us:

1. Leadership tasks are never finished. As change agents, we remain part of the process.
2. Our thoughts and processes display integrity only if our lifestyle is congruous with those thoughts and processes. This means that it's not what we *do* as much as who we *are*. We shift the emphasis from *doing* to *being*. Just as leaders enter a different level of leadership when they move from *projects* (what) to *people* (who).

Futuring: Leading Your Church into Tomorrow invites you to take this exciting journey where the little creature from the film *ET* can't take you—but God can.

Afterword

Dr. John C. Maxwell

When I study leadership, especially in church and church-related ministries, I am often surprised by the lack of intentional and deliberate planning for the future. I want to encourage you to reflect on what you have just finished reading. *Futuring: Leading Your Church into Tomorrow* reminds us that change is not an option, but we do have choices when it comes to how we react to change. By reflecting and acting on Dr. Chand's words, you can choose to proactively respond to the changing horizon. You can intentionally and deliberately plan for your future and the future of your ministry.

Along with Dr. Chand's insightful and practical information, there are three things I urge you to think about and put into action:

1. *Remind* yourself that the future is already here.
2. *Watch* the emerging trends (chapter 14).
3. *Study* the five major appeals (chapter 15).

The Future Is Here

To get different results, we must do different things. But all too often I see people jump into an approach or method simply because of its newness. They become fad followers. Churches that want to thrive won't buy into trends just for the sake of their novelty. Instead, thoughtful futurefaith leaders will know why they want to do things differently. They will ask, "How will this affect us now and in the days ahead?"

The future is not an ambiguous entity out there. The future is already knocking on your door as you read this book. This leaves you with a question: "Now what?"

Watch the Emerging Trends

Emerging trends prepare us for relevant leadership. As I talk to leaders all over the world, I often feel like asking, "Didn't you see it coming? How could you have missed it?" Maybe they miss trends because they are not intentionally looking for them.

> Check your tool belt. It's heavier now than when you began to read this book, isn't it?

New ways of framing the world are always emerging, communication patterns stay in flux, and leadership is asserted in new ways. Not to keep a watchful eye is like repairing today's automobile with tools used for cars made thirty years ago. If we work hard with fevered energy with those tools, we can make the vehicle run—although not well. We exert maximum effort but get minimal results.

This book equips you with the up-to-date tools you will need to do your job today and tomorrow. Use these tools to identify trends in your ministry and community.

Study the Five Major Appeals

Dr. Chand lists the five major appeals as compassion, community, challenge, reasonability, and commitment. These are the appeals that lead people into action. If you, as a futurefaith leader, decide on your appeal, customize your approach, and create a plan, you can change from being a drifting church to a strong, growing, intentional congregation.

If you want to be a futurefaith leader and want your church to flourish, make sure leaders on every level within your sphere of influence also know and understand these principles. Equip them and allow them to come alongside of you as together you prepare your church for the future.

Samuel Chand is one of the brightest lights on the horizon of the Church today.

Jack Hayford, Van Nuys, California

When Samuel Chand speaks, I listen. When he writes, I read what he has to say. You will do well to do so too.

Vinson Synan, Regent University, Virginia Beach, Virginia

He epitomizes the aphorism: "Leadership begins with vision, and vision is a holy discontent with things as they are."

Ray Bakke, International Urban Associates, Seattle, Washington

Dr. Chand will guide you through the steps necessary to position you and your church for growth. I highly recommend *Futuring* as a must-read for leaders.

Jim Bolin, Trinity Chapel, Powder Springs, Georgia

He is a vision caster, a bridge builder, and a change agent . . . The result is Kingdom change.

David Allman, Regent Partners, Atlanta, Georgia

Dr. Samuel Chand is a person I consult when planning a trip to the land of tomorrow. He has lived most of his life there, and is superbly suited to help you plan your excursion from today into your tomorrow.

Bishop Clyde M. Hughes, International Pentecostal Church of
Christ, London, Ohio

I am truly impressed with his understanding and appreciation of cross-cultural dynamics as it relates to the church.

Frank Alexander, Oasis of Hope Baptist Church,
Indianapolis, Indiana

Dr. Chand brings clear-cut leadership to the local church. He is on the cutting edge.

Stephen Green Sr., More than Conquerors Faith Church,
Birmingham, Alabama

We must step out of our gilded boxes of complacency to address the necessity of change. Sam Chand's radical approach and passion gives us direction.

Collette L. Gunby, Green Pastures Christian Ministries, Inc., Decatur, Georgia

Dr. Chand is both a leader and a change agent—vitally aware of the mission of the church in a changing world.

Dr. Carolyn Tennant, North Central University, Minneapolis, Minnesota

The American society continues to change while many Christian leaders seem frozen in a past age. Samuel Chand has a focus on the future. He is an energetic visionary.

A. Charles Ware, Crossroads Bible College, Indianapolis, Indiana

He has done what few others have been able to do in crossing the ethnic lines of the church.

Randy Valimont, First Assembly of God, Griffin, Georgia

What Dr. Chand is experiencing now, the rest of us will experience soon.

Thomas R. Roddy, Atlanta Resource Foundation, Atlanta, Georgia

His insight to see farther than others is a gift from God, and he has a servant's heart to share it with others.

Roger D. Mileham, Trinity Family Worship Center, Rex, Georgia

He sees beyond today and touches tomorrow.

Tom Mullins, Christ Fellowship Church, Palm Beach Gardens, Florida

He draws together divergent people of faith, inspires them with a common vision, and mobilizes them to unified action.

Bob Lupton, FCS Ministries, Atlanta, Georgia

He has his finger on the pulse of Christ's church and his ear tuned to the voice of the Father.

Walter F. Harvey, Parklawn Assembly of God,
Milwaukee, Wisconsin

Dr. Chand's assignment in life is clearly to develop the church in unprecedented ways into what God has destined it to be at such a time as this.

Cynthia L. Hale, Ray of Hope Christian Church, Decatur, Georgia

The way he integrates the dynamics of his themes by simplifying, challenging, and promoting application is astonishing.

Jerry D. Fryar, Gospel Lighthouse Church, Columbus, Ohio

A change agent. No progress is possible unless we allow ourselves to be changed. In everything he does, Chand imparts vision for what is possible if we are willing to change.

Doug Chatham, Atlanta, Georgia

Sam has great insights on leadership for today's pastors. Good commonsense wisdom from above.

Dr. David C. Cooper, Senior Pastor, Mount Paran Church of God,
Atlanta, Georgia

Dr. Chand is an emerging voice in the arena of church leadership development. He challenges the church to be relevant and effective to the times. His voice is refreshing and thought provoking.

Tony Morris, Senior Leader, New Covenant Christian Center,
Seattle, Washington

About Dr. Samuel R. Chand

As a *Dream Releaser,* Sam Chand serves pastors, ministries, and businesses as a leadership architect and change strategist. He is a popular and much sought after speaker for churches, corporations, leadership and ministry conferences, and other leadership development seminars.

In 1973, while a student at Beulah Heights Bible College, Sam Chand served as janitor, cook, and dishwasher. He graduated and was ordained in the ministry in 1977 and went on to serve as an associate and senior pastor in several churches. Sixteen years later, he returned to BHBC to serve as the president for the next 14 years. Under his leadership, BHBC became one of the fastest growing bible colleges in America experiencing a 600% increase in student growth, an enrollment of approximately 700 students from over 400 churches, 45 denominations, and 32 countries. Beulah Heights Bible College is also the country's largest predominantly African-American Bible college. He also served the school as chancellor.

Currently, Dr. Chand ...

- Consults with businesses and large churches on leadership and capacity enhancing issues
- Conducts nation-wide leadership conferences
- Presents at international leadership conferences with Dr. John Maxwell's ministry of EQUIP
- Serves on the board of EQUIP, with the goal to equip 50 million leaders worldwide

- Oversees and leads Bishop Eddie L. Long's leadership development initiatives through Father's House, Spirit & Truth and other leadership development events
- Is on the Board of Faith Academy, an accredited Christian school
- Works as a facilitator of African-American Consortium of Theological Studies (AACTS), a ministry in Kenya to bring collaboration and leadership development to bear upon major churches, denominations and government in Kenya
- Dr. Chand has authored and published five books, which are used worldwide for leadership development. His books include:

What's Shakin' Your Ladder: 15 Challenges All Leaders Face advice for leaders on how to overcome the things that are blocking them.

Who Moved Your Ladder: Your Next Bold Move This book provides pragmatic guidelines for dealing with transitions in life and leadership.

Who's Holding Your Ladder A reminder to that the most critical decision leaders will make is selecting who will be on their leadership team.

FUTURING: Leading your Church into Tomorrow This book is helps leaders to begin a future oriented dialog about their organization.

Failure: The Womb of Success a compilation of stories on how to overcome failure with contributions from twenty respected Christian leaders.

Chand's educational background includes an honorary Doctor of Divinity from Heritage Bible College, a Master of Arts in Biblical Counseling from Grace Theological Seminary, a Bachelor of Arts in Biblical Education from Beulah Heights Bible College.

Dr. Chand shares his life and love with his wife Brenda, two daughters Rachel and Deborah and granddaughter Adeline.

Being raised in a pastor's home in India has uniquely equipped Dr. Chand to share his passion – that of mentoring, developing and inspiring leaders to break all limits—in ministry and the marketplace.

For further information please contact:

Samuel R. Chand Ministries, Inc.
950 Eagles Landing Parkway, Suite 295
Stockbridge, GA 30281
770-898-6464
www.samchand.com

LEADERSHIP RESOURCES
BY SAMUEL R. CHAND

FUTURING:
Leading Your Church into Tomorrow

> The message will never change. But the methods to present the message can and must change to reach a realm of churchgoers. Forty-four specific areas that are changing in the church today.

WHO'S HOLDING YOUR LADDER?
Leadership's Most Critical Decision —Selecting Your Leaders

> Those around you, not you, the visionary, will determine your success.

WHO MOVED YOUR LADDER?
Your Next Bold Move

> Taking the next bold move is not easy— but you finally admit, "I have no choice. I have to jump!"
>
> This book will equip you for that leap.

WHAT'S SHAKIN' YOUR LADDER?
15 Challenges All Leaders Face

> Take an in-depth look at the common challenges that all leaders face, and benefit from practical advice on facing and overcoming the things that are blocking you from being the best you can be.

CHANGE:
Leading Change Effectively

- Healthy confessions for those leading change
- Tradition and traditionalism
- Responding to seasons and times
- Levels of change
- Factors that facilitate or hinder change
- Steps for positive change
- Selling your idea
- Creating a team
- Personal challenges of the leader leading change

Developing a Leadership Culture

- Why do leaders do what they do?
- Why and when leaders make changes?
- Vision levels of people
- Contemporary leadership
- Why leaders fail
- Qualities of a successful leader

FAILURE:
The Womb of Success

- Failure is an event not a person
- Failure is never final
- Twenty leaders tell their stories

Formation of a Leader

Spiritual Formation
- Born to lead
- Security or sabotage

Skill Formation
- The day Moses became a leader

Strategic Formation
- Live the life you were meant to live
- Mentoring: How to invest your life in others

FUTURING:
Leading Your Church Into Tomorrow

- Futuring leadership traits
- Challenges for the 21st century
- How ministry will change in the next 3-7 years
- Motivational fuels for 21st century church
- Addition versus multiplication of leaders

12 Success Factors for an Organization

- Handling Complexity
- Completion
- Lead and Manage People
- Executional Excellence

What Keeps Pastors Up At Night

- Do my people get the vision?
- Are things getting done?
- How is the team working together?
- Do I have the team I need to get it done?

Who's Holding Your Ladder?

- Ladder holders determine the Leader's ascent
- Selecting your ladder holders
- Different ladder holders for different levels
- Qualities of a good ladder holder
- Development of ladder holders
- Leaders versus Managers
- Turning ladder holders into ladder climbers

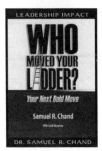

Who Moved Your Ladder?
Your Next Bold Move

- What's wrong with me?
- What's wrong with my ladder?
- What's going on?
- What happened to the challenge?
- Where's the thrill of achievement?

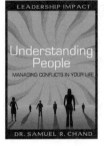

Understanding People:

Managing Conflicts in Your Ministry

- What conflict does
- High maintenance relationships
- Predictable times of conflict
- Levels of conflict
- Diffusing conflict
- Conflict resolution

HOW TO ORDER RESOURCES

CALL
770-898-6464

WRITE
Samuel R. Chand Ministries
950 Eagles Landing Parkway, Suite 295
Stockbridge, GA 30281

WEBSITE
www.samchand.com

NOTES
1. BULK purchase (10 or more) rates available.
2. Credit cards & checks accepted

NOTES

NOTES

NOTES

Notes

NOTES

Notes